THE BEDOUINS
OF ARABIA

Thierry MAUGER

Translated from the French by
Khia MASON and Igor PERSAN

Souffles, *Création, production, édition*
28, Boulevard de Strasbourg, 75010 Paris, France
Tél : (33) (1) 42 03 22 33. Télex : 240 934 F.

© Souffles, S.A., October 1987
ISBN : 2-87658-019-5
First english edition : April 1988

Acknowledgements.

I would like to thank the following individuals for the generous hospitality bestowed on me in Yabrin during my prolonged stay in Arabia : Prince Hamad Bin Jaber Al-Murdif Al-MURRY, Mohammad Bin Hamad Al-MURRY, Saeed Mohammad Al-MURRY, Mohammad Bin Hawai Al-Shamaly Al-MURRY and Fuhaid Bin Hujaim Al-Saddada Al-MURRY.

I am deeply grateful to the Bedouins of all the tribes of Arabia. Although I left with no plans to return, these people will nevertheless remain in my heart and mind.

I thank Dorothée BURKEL, François DIAB, Jean-Michel GUERIN, Christiane LANGEL and Claudine MAUGER, who kindly donated their precious time and advice.

I also thank THOMSON-CSF for its participation and encouragement.
And, above all, I would like to thank my wife Danielle, who, whilst among the Bedouins, continually spoke from her heart.

"THE MEMORIES OF A NATION
LEAVE A SCAR ;
IF CHEATED WITH,
THEY BECOME NOTHING BUT TATTOOS"
(Jean MAUGER)

Author's note.

I have used Arabic words that belong to a past way of life. In order to avoid heaviness in the text, I have simplified the phonetic transcription by dispensing with diacritical signs and keeping to the singular. Purists will certainly propose alternatives that they consider more faithful to the beauty of the sound of Arabic.

The quoted verses are translated from the original French translation by Albert LENTIN of "L'éloge de la vie bédouine" by Emir Abd Al-QADER.

"WORDS WEAR OUT,
AS DO THE THINGS THEY DESCRIBE"

Publisher's note.

The publishing team would like to express its gratitude for the perseverance of Madame Danielle MAUGER during the long and difficult hours spent on this undertaking. Without her contribution, this book would never have seen the light of day.

Foreword.

This is the story of two meetings.
One with a country - Saudi Arabia, another with a people
- the Bedouins.
The first meeting came about in the course of my profes-
sional activity. The second was the result of personal interest and a lively curiosity.

It is too simplistic to think of this country, dominated by
desert, as just a vast expanse of sand where, several thousand years ago, a movement of nomadic pastoralism - as
is still practiced today - was born.

The word bedouin signifies, in its strictest sense, nomad
of the desert. Today, in this region, it applies to anyone
who practices pastoral activities.

Bedouins came partly from the North -Arab descendants
of Adnan - and partly from the sons of Qahtan in the
South. The foundation of their genealogy has its roots in
the eponymic ancestor and remains their only durable
source of transmissible knowledge.
Whether they came from the North or the South, all
Bedouins are nevertheless organized under one common
tribal system. The severe conditions of pastoral nomadic
life do not favour heavy demographic concentration. Tribes are dispersed according to clan, lineage and extended
family but nevertheless retain a common lineage.

Since 1932, when the legendary Abdul Aziz Ibn Saoud
assembled the tribes under one banner and created the
Kingdom of Saudi Arabia, all its inhabitants have become
Saudi citizens.

Although today nation takes precedence over tribe, the
country is still a mosaic of tribes welded together by the
tremendous cohesive force of a common inspiration :
Islam.

The destiny of the Kingdom has altered considerably
since the onset of oil mining in 1938. The major indus-
trialization that followed on from this "gift of Allah"
swiftly brought prosperity to this hostile land.

For the first time the Bedouins are confronted with the
mythical salvation of modernism. Moreover, the recent
introduction of televisions infects these people with the
virus of another world's idealism.

The more they come under the grip of the western world, the greater their difficulty in accepting the rigours of the desert : their needs, and consequently their obligations and their burden, increase. Even their sense of hospitality, of style, their basic needs and desires has lost its edge.

I was particularly struck by the increasing fragility of the Bedouins' heritage, the very thing that binds together the Saudi nation, and I have felt a necessity to transmit what I had witnessed : the extinction of a civilization.

The main interest surrounding the Bedouins lies in their ability to adapt to the extremes of desert life and to the fact that they have drawn their livelihood almost exclusively from the dromedary, the animal which, according to the Prophet, is the most perfect achievement in God's Creation.

This book is not a detailed catalogue of Bedouin tribes, neither is it an ethnological thesis. It is simply a collection of privileged moments that my wife Danielle and I spent amongst a people who accepted us and eventually won us over completely...

Before sharing this slice of Bedouin life with the reader, I would like to emphasize an extremely important point -it is much easier to gain the trust of desert tribes-people when travelling as a couple.

A man on his own would find it impossible to make intimate contact with a family, thus Danielle's importance to this long quest. Another point : anthropomorphic representation is forbidden by the faith of a good number of iconophobic Bedouins. Initially, the categoric refusal of any form of photographic activity seemed an insurmountable obstacle. However, my patience and obstinacy helped me to put together a substantial collection of photographs, the only way to capture the essence of a dying civilization.

Some geographical and political considerations.

Saudi Arabia covers an area of approximately 2,150,000 km² - an immense stretch of barren land covering most of the Arabian Peninsula.

To the West is the sandy coastal strip of Tihama flanked by the Hedjaz Mountains. This ridge gives access to high plateaux leading on to the Najd tableland, sloping gently down to the East as far as the al Hasa plain on the Arabian Gulf. It is here on the Gulf that abound the prosperous oil wells and oases. The North of the country is closed off by the Nafud Desert.

With its plentiful rainfall, the south-western mountainous region of Assir espaces the harsh climate endured by the rest of the country. To the South, its borders merge with the sands of the mighty Rub al Khali Desert.

Saudi Arabia is a monarchy established on the principles of predominantly Sunnite Islam. This austere and stringent form of Islamic faith is known as Wahabinism.

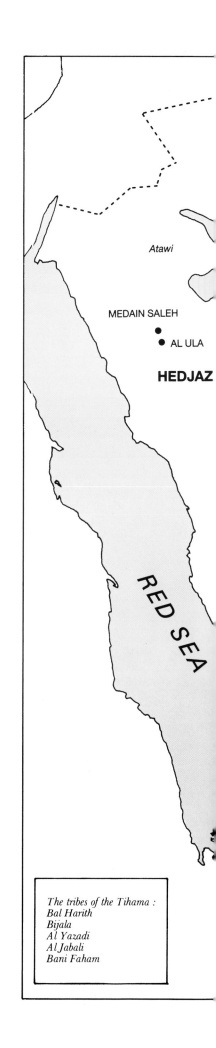

Atawi

MEDAIN SALEH
● AL ULA

HEDJAZ

RED SEA

The tribes of the Tihama :
Bal Harith
Bijala
Al Yazadi
Al Jabali
Bani Faham

12

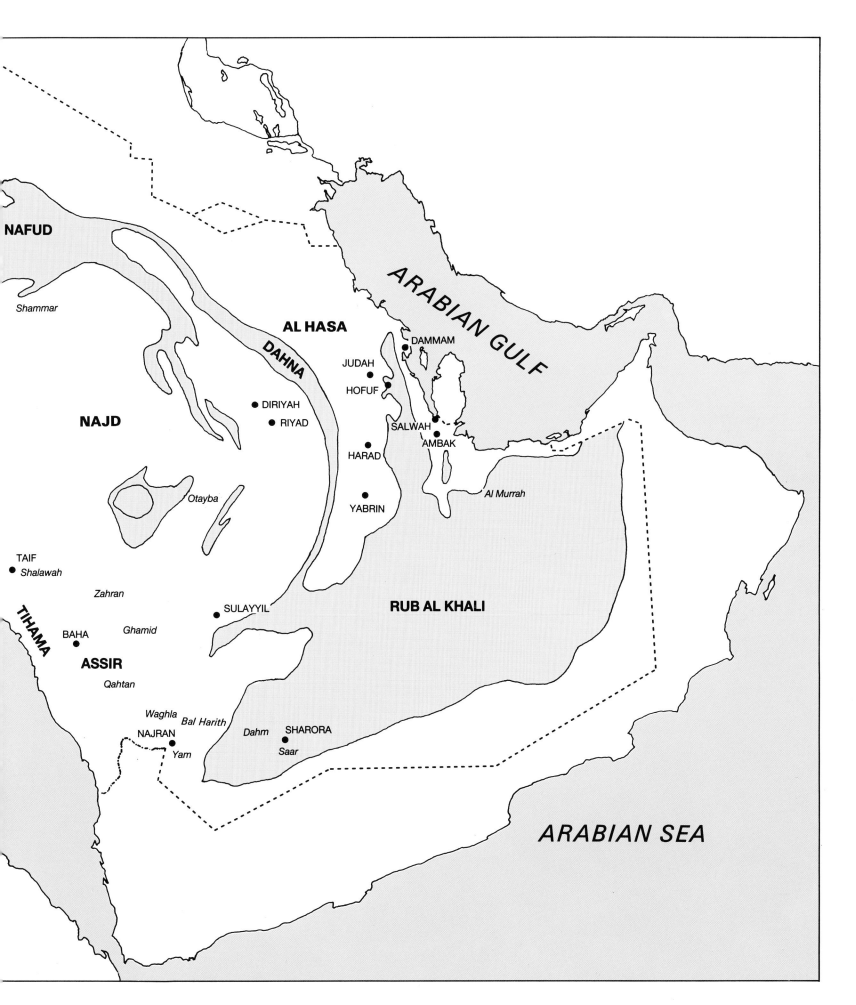

NAFUD

Shammar

AL HASA

DAHNA

NAJD

DIRIYAH

RIYAD

Otayba

ARABIAN GULF

DAMMAM

JUDAH

HOFUF

SALWAH

AMBAK

HARAD

YABRIN

Al Murrah

TAIF

Shalawah

Zahran

SULAYYIL

RUB AL KHALI

TIHAMA

BAHA

Ghamid

ASSIR

Qahtan

Waghla

Bal Harith

Dahm

SHARORA

NAJRAN

Yam

Saar

ARABIAN SEA

En route for Najran.

"You see arid land, but give it water and instantly it stirs, it swells and every kind of plant blossoms forth".
(The Koran, XXII,5)

The itinerary we are to follow derives its logic from the country's geography. A distance of 1000 km lies between Taif, our home-base and Najran, the last southern outpost before reaching Yemen.
Earlier geological movement in the area that is now covered by the Red Sea pushed up high mountain ranges on its banks. To the East, these ranges become the Sarawat Mountains. The Assir, as this south-western corner of Arabia is known, has been spared the extreme drought that ravages the rest of the country. Along the length of this ridge, the air mass from the Red Sea rises abruptly then cools down, bringing regular life-giving rains to the land. Although agricultural life is more widespread than nomadic pastoralism, most tribes are semi-nomadic.

Families are established in a village, some of their members working the land, living Bedouin-style under the tent whilst others graze their herds nearby. Nomadic and sedentary lifestyles complement one another ; the Bedouins maintain contacts with oasis-dwellers and peasants for trading purposes.

The escarpment we are following provides staggering views of mist-covered depths. From each new bend in the road we can see, silhouetted high on the ridges, massive stone walls interrupted by watch-towers.
Staggered terraced gardens on the slopes suggest yet another side of Arabia.

Najran.

Najran, an exquisite oasis, for a long time considered a major stop-over on the incense and myrrh routes, has everything to delight the weary traveller's eye. "An oasis after the desert is certainty after doubt, life after the void".

It is also greenness after sand, the hard lines of palm trees after soft curving dunes and it is the generosity of irrigation pumps feeding the canals contrasted with the permanent dryness of empty spaces.

The oasis was once a gathering-place and a port of call for caravans. Here, the date-palm predominates, as it does on the national flag, where - together with two swords - it symbolizes the alliance of prosperity and justice.

We wander through the **souk**, close to the old Government House. Each Friday, it attracts neighbouring tribes who come to buy anything and everything. The market square jostles with the lengthy diatribe of glib-tongued vendors and their prospective clients. Tradition dictates that profit remains a secondary consideration when bargaining – precedence always being given to the game. The Najran **souk** owes its reputation to its jewelry, its craft-work and the diversity of its products. Our senses are tantalized by the profusion of colours and smells of the many spices. Overflowing baskets are attractively arranged side by side with flasks of perfume brought by the, now motorized, caravans. Lying on the ground are skin-bags - **okka** - bursting with **samn**, the precious clarified butter.

Danielle is attracted by the jewelry and she spies a silver triangle set off by a red stone - **lawh**. After some keen bargaining, she buys a **mazab** - a saffron-coloured cradle with a heady odour of goat.

An artisan is sharpening a **jambaya** -the curved dagger worn vertically in the centre of the waist-belt, the glans of its silver sheath adding to the imagery of an erect phallus - symbol of virility and courage.

Clusters of dates, like red, yellow and brown tears, spill over the sides of pick-up trucks. This royal fruit contains large amounts of sugar and when dried, can be kept for long periods. They are always served with coffee under the tent. It is high noon and the sun is at its most intense. The prayer call cuts short our bargaining. The market-place empties and not a sound can be heard as we leave. The best way to discover is to allow oneself to be guided by the simple magic of the place.

After the enchantment of the **souk** we come across elegant traditional houses under the palms. **Najrani** architecture is a fine example of Southern Arabia's craftsmanship. Wetted earth mixed with straw or palm cuttings is used as a building material. Wads of this mixture are placed one on top of the other to construct thick walls which retain the heat in winter and the cool in summer. Despite these remarkable characteristics, the new generation of builders is turning more and more from this material - mistakenly considered obsolete - toward the construction of comfortable but ugly accommodation. In a region where it was once constantly necessary to be protected from invading Bedouins, many farms were fortified. Some of these - no longer serving as fortresses - are still used as accommodation.

Desert people lead an extremely convivial life.

This Qahtan herdswoman wears her silver crown like a princess.

A solemn and patriarchal posture upholds the father's authority.(page 21)

All southern Arabs proudly wear the "khanjar", a symbol of their masculinity. (page 21)

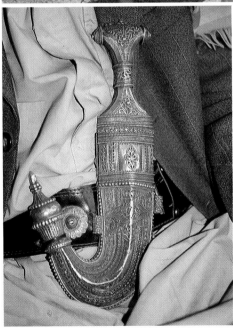

Suddenly, we are attacked and harassed by a swarm of hornets. Stoically, Danielle endures the pain of several stings. We have heard that eight can be fatal ! A young boy turns up at the right time and leads us to a pharmacy, then - once Danielle has recovered - he invites us to his home.

The footwear cluttering the step is a sure sign that people are inside. Entering, we are struck by the lavishness of the decor. The women have an inborn feeling for primary colours ; walls, stairways and ceilings are painted with alternating bands of red, yellow, blue and green. A constant delight to the eye !
The house has been arranged according to the requirements of Moslem life. One room is used to entertain guests and the other - the **harem** - is strictly reserved for the womenfolk. We settle in the former, where some young girls pay us their respects then quickly disappear.

Very little furniture is needed by these people, who are accustomed to sitting on the ground. There are rugs on the floor and arm-rests are arranged at regular intervals around the walls. We are served tea, a daily ceremony respected by all Saudis.

We move into the garden where our host displays his pleasure by honouring us with a gift of fruit.
Taking our leave, we continue our stroll through the palm-grove. Occasionally we see towers looming up in the corner of a field - they were once used as barns or as a shelter from invaders.
Now, children climb those towers that are still in reasonable repair to aim their murderous catapults at the birds.

An occasional small group of dromedaries reminds us of another way of life, that of the nomads. These familiar beasts that once roamed the wide desert spaces, are now kept in small compounds - made even smaller as the cereal crops take over more space. Their numbers dwindle yearly as the number of vehicles increases.
With the recent arrival of this mode of transport, the dromedary often spends its life as a "milking cow" or finishes it under the butcher's knife. Arab poets no longer sing the praises of this remarkable animal "with sad eyes, framed by long and languorous lashes". The petrol pump takes over where poetry left off.

Many of the redeployed Bedouins still retain a taste for adventure and the open spaces. What better to satisfy these deeply-rooted needs than the driver's seat of a heavy Mercedes, trucking across the country. Yesterday it was the caravan, today it is the truck. Behind the wheel there is a sense of freedom and no need for clock-watching. Only the form has changed. Gaily decked with bright colours, dripping with chrome and embellished with naive frescoes, this mechanical horse is a noisy replacement for the silent "ship of the desert" - the splendidly harnessed camel of another era.
A pick-up truck passes us, enveloped in a cloud of dust and overflowing with women, children and animals. This contemporary Noah's ark sags under its load. With each violent jerk, the passengers are jostled one against the other, hanging on for dear life to the side-rails as if to the reins of a bolting horse.

Three splashes of colour : the world of the Qahtan woman. (page 22)

A Qahtan woman rekindles the fire under the ashes. (page 23)

Young Yam girls from the Rub al Khali wear a mask from the age of seven. (page 23)

The Qahtan half-mask heavy with silver

On the western fringe of the Rub al Khali.

The desert stands at the very edge of the city. Cutting its way through, the highway traces a long black line, broken here and there by gusts of sand. A sudden swirl sucks up everything in its path and whips up the inert road into a sudden frenzy of activity, only to die a few hundred yards further on. The battle of the jinns has ended.

Acacia trees thrust out their umbrellas, offering nature's toothpicks to the passer-by. Dusty, bleached-out scraps of material are carried by the wind to hang from their flimsy thorns. This organic barbed-wire does not, however, discourage the goats or dromedaries from feasting on their tips. The glossy-leafed **ushar** - a curious shrub with bulbous flowers - completes the scene. Its flora, incongruous in this parched land, struggles to put on a bright face to remind us that life is omnipresent.
The friendly, docile donkeys enjoy scraps of food tossed from passing cars then sprawl out on the ground with their heads bowed low as if they belonged to some contemplative order.

Our tank needs to be topped up at the last filling station, before heading into the desert. Sitting on high benches in the local "tea rooms", men are sucking on the **shisha** - a long-stemmed water-pipe, convivially passed from mouth to mouth like a peacepipe. Whilst they enjoy this "silent companion with its red eye and fever in its belly", others play **kerum** - a type of billiards. The players must drop the pieces into a pocket through a series of flips and rebounds. Close by, a herd of goats happily busy themselves with refuse collection duties. In their struggle to survive, they show a remarkable capacity for adapting to the "wealth" of the environment. Their craving for paper comes from the ability of their digestive system to combine nitrogen and cellulose, thereby creating protein.

Past and present interact. A dromedary is lashed to the back of a small truck -its heavy, fat hump suggesting a Mr. Punch. Here we see the reality - the end of the dromedary as a means of transport.
A stinking heap of skin and bones on the roadside symbolizes the constant drama played out between man and animal. A bird of prey hovers and then spirals down towards to the dead beast. How many Bedouins have met their end behind the wheel when, drunk with speed, they smash into one of their ancient companions ?
For many of these people, the automobile is an outlet for the energy once released in razzias and tribal wars. Technology rules in the desert, breaking up the way of life that was once centered around the camel.

A Bani Faham woman churns butter in a skin bag suspended from a tripod.

The convivial world of a Bedouin family. (page 28)

A ceremonial head-dress, a fine example of Tihama craft-work. (page 29)

In the Rub al Khali.

The bushy steppes give way to gentle undulations, and then to the majestic dunes that give the ergs their appeal. We are on the edge of the famed Rub al Khali, Arabia's southernmost desert whose name signifies "empty quarter". It is uninhabited except for occasional Bedouins, soldiers and a few prospectors. However, legend says that it is peopled by jinns, demons and other malevolent spirits. Seldom has any mortal dared to risk the hazards of this vast scorching place, as big as France. Although for many, the Rub al Khali is Hell's Antechamber, for some, it holds an irresistible attraction. Nobody felt its pull more than Wilfred Thesiger. Once almost impenetrable, this desert to end all deserts can now be partially crossed by road.

On either side of the road protruding bitumen defiles the purity of the sands in order to hold back the shifting dunes. The tiniest details stand out in the emptiness of the surrounding desert. Animal tracks and their droppings are the only signs of life. With no wood to burn, the smokeless and odourless camel manure makes an elegant fuel. After drying and crushing, its highly absorbent quality makes it an ideal replacement for the disposable-diaper when packed at the bottom of a child's cot.
What better place than here to contemplate infinity. As far as the eye can see, the dunes roll on for ever in their geometric curves. This endlessly repetitive landscape can bring on vertigo, but once this passes, the senses are liberated, the soul purged.
The dunes are formed when wind and sand meet, the former sculpting the latter with a vigorous hand. The wind drives the sand, it swells and blows up in waves rising and falling, one against the other, pushing the horizon back even further.

The windward side of the dune is rimmed by a convex crescent. The other side is hollowed out as the sand slips away. A changing wind sends the dunes into a flurry of confusion. Cutting across this labyrinth are corridors that afford easy access for camp-seeking nomads.
The Bedouin is guided by his interpretation of the environment, his observation of wind, sun and stars. He is gifted with a remarkable memory for the lie of the land.
The **aabal**, a green shrub sprouts up out of the sand. In Spring, its scarlet fruit revives the desert. According to the Bedouins, this plant can resist several years of drought.

After travelling alone for several hours, various signs start to betray the presence of people. Here and there -like driftwood - part of a saddle, a worn tyre. Car tracks, crisscrossing like tracks in a marshalling yard, mark out the semblance of a path that will eventually lead to an encampment.
I forget time, I forget the car and I nurse the impossible hope of meeting up with a caravan. The desert summons up a flood of clichés - stubbornly feeding my nostalgia for a romantic world.
The dark outline of a herd of goats interrupts this short-lived fantasy. The young goatherd leading them appears, as if from out of the mists of time - a time when man and animal lived together in harmony.

An age-old activity : spinning by the Al Yazadi of the Tihama

Prestigious adornment worn by the Bani Faham goatherds throughout her daily chores.

Precarious living in the hostile environment of the Tihama.(p.32)

Nostalgic for his past deeds. Zahran of the Tihama. (page 33)

I cut the engine so as not to frighten off some peacefully grazing dromedaries. They turn their heads, fixing us with that look which could well come from their reaction to our presence, but it is also from the high position of their nostrils in relation to their eyes. A curl of their lip and they amble off. I go to follow them on foot, but my feet sink into the sand. It is a problem they do not have with their broad soles. As soon as they sense a respectable distance between us, they relax and continue majestically on their way.

Capable of survival in the most difficult conditions, these evolutionary wonders proudly possess, not only the secrets of the desert, but also - according to an Arab proverb - knowledge of Allah's one hundredth attribute.
The dromedary's quest for survival is motivated by its hump - indicator of its relative strength or weakness. It can only be replenished by the scanty vegetation nurtured by the sporadic and highly localized rainfall.

A short while later, three tents appear on the horizon, like giant bats clawing at the ground. Made from woven goat hair, the tents - **bayt al shaar** - give the impression that they have been blackened by the sun.
This fluid architectural style, for ever linked to nomadic life, stretches from Mauritania - through Afghanistan - to Tibet. It is, quite evidently, born from a blend of necessity, availability of material and aesthetic awareness - a universally valid formula !
Camps are organized according to lineage ; with the tents positioned to avoid the insolent rays of the scorching sun.
The Rub al Khali is the domain of the nomadic herdsman. Its limited resources can only support a restricted number of livestock and soon becomes overcrowded ! Encampments are dispersed in such way as to maintain a respectable distance between each other.

These men live out their existence in constant defiance of the desert's oppressive heat, infertile ground and culpable sky. Looking out over this arid land, we eventually wonder how the Bedouins can ever live here. The desert gives no quarter to an impostor - the Bedouins must go with the flow, as naturally as birds migrate. A dignified, contented life is just as possible here as it is in an urbanized world. There is always, of course, the darker side - the hardship and privation resulting from the climate. This, however, is the price the nomad pays for freedom.

A Bal Harith tribesman, Tihama (p. 35)

The fragrances of Arabia rise out from a small container. Al Jabali of the Tihama.

The Yam Bedouins.

We take advantage of our privilege as strangers and enter the confines of the camp. Underfoot, animal droppings cover the ground making crunching sounds. Here, hospitality is sacrosanct and the traveller, far from home, can always find food and shelter.

For three days, this even applies to an enemy who, on penetrating a tent, becomes its symbolic master.

We always make sure that there is at least one man in the encampment - otherwise the women are likely send us away, unless that is, Danielle gains their confidence.

Some goats in search of shade shuffle under our car. We pass by a tent. Silence... but eyes are doubtlessly peering at us from within.

A welcome sight in this sun-bleached landscape are the gaily coloured bowser-trucks, with gleaming tanks holding the water that is so precious to the Bedouins. Tradition and modernity constantly blend and clash - an anachronism that ethnologists call "acculturation", but which Wilfred Thesiger more coldly names "materialistic profanation". Sacks of barley, intended for the animals, are stacked in pyramids, a guarantee of security, insurance against drought and the first step in the settling process.

A horde of children swarms all over us and then lead us to the most impressive tent. It is surprisingly large, far bigger than the tent of the Shalawah* to which we had become accustomed. Long ropes hold the lightly sloping roof against the wind. From one of them is hanging a skein of freshly dyed wool, drying in the sun. The tent's roof and sides are made from long strips of material that the women weave loosely enough to ensure good ventilation

before stitching them together. The thread expands with the rain, making the tent waterproof. Cross-strips, decorated with geometrical motifs, are stretched between the tent poles to support the roof. The number of poles is an indication of the owner's power or wealth. The wall - **hijab** - is attached to the roof with large iron needles, so that, should the wind decide to change, it can be easily relocated. The tent is cooled by an assiduously maintained draught of air -referred to ironically by the Bedouins as their "air-conditioning".

Sitting by the threshold of the tent, gazing into infinity, is the patriarch, sublimely unconcerned with the anguish of his times. His walk-worn, calloused feet have no need of sandals. His desert-wise eyes, seared by the sun, are filled with yearning for a timeless dream. His lips move incessantly in a subdued and timorous soliloquy. He seems to be lost in another world.

Inside the tent, a woman is weaving. Not far from her side, a baby is lying, wrapped and bound like an Egyptian mummy, in a magnificent cradle fashioned from a brick-coloured leather, dyed with **samra** resin. The child will stay bound like this for the first few months of its life, in order to acquire a good posture.

A small half-naked boy with a leather thong - **subta** - around his waist, is staring at us with his jet-black eyes. Round his neck is a cloth collar with pieces of basil and the protective cauris* at either end. His sister watches the weaving, practicing on a miniature replica of her mother's loom. In this way, she also is taking part in the life of the encampment.

The children's education starts early and progresses naturally with the help

* A nomadic tribe in the Taif region

* Cauris - shells of the porcelain group

In the heart of the Najran oasis traditional architecture still catches the eye.

Explosion of colours in a Qahtan oasis dweller's house (p. 40-41)

of oral instruction. Quickly, they become initiated into the adult's world. The father instills them with a knowledge of their ancestry, the Koran being assimilated through constant repetition and long evenings are spent listening to the patriarch's stories and poems, to develop an outstanding memory. However, the children soon stop seeking the elders' advice, they forsake their gestures and discover Scholarship...

In these modern times, childhood is very short-lived. The youngsters do not have many games or toys. Dunes are their sandcastles, live animals their fluffy toys and the firearms are very real. Younger brothers and sisters take the place of dolls. They quickly move on to more adult activities, helping their parents with daily chores. In return, they are lavished with an affection that is unrivalled elsewhere.

I can only observe family activity from a distance - a distance that must be kept between an outsider and the women.
Danielle squats down near the weaver, without interrupting the work. In a society concerned for its reputation, the poorly rewarded and arduous textile work is perhaps the best illustration of Bedouin craft, where things of great beauty are often produced with the scantiest of means.
A unique, horizontal, single-warp loom is used. It is collapsible and easily carried, even with work in progress still on the loom. It is constructed from materials at hand, parts are easily replaced. Its narrow construction imposes the oblong shape of the work produced - roofs, walls, rugs and dividers. Working on this sort of loom requires strength and dexterity. The woman adjusts yarn tension with help

from her big-toe. Accustomed to living close to the ground, the foot is used quite naturally as a third hand.

Each time the shuttle moves across, she vigorously packs down the yarn with the help of a flat stick, glossy from long use, then untangles the skein with a goat-horn.
The taboo on figurative representation serves as a pretext for the creation of a diversity of beautiful geometrical motifs symbolizing various objects by lines, hachures and dots in a completely abstract form. Age-old gestures, passed down from mother to daughter, take precedence over a highly conscious aesthetic.
Natural colourings once dictated the choice of colours. Nowadays, the yellows, reds and browns - much brighter because of the introduction of artificial additives - have lost their original warmth.

Skilled fingers silently run over the instrument's many strings, producing a **ruag** - a divider used to separate the men's quarters - **majilis** - from the women's. The Bedouin's skill and creativity produces its finest expression in these huge "tapestries". The finished screen, with its subtle motifs provides a safeguard against male inquisitiveness. Deliberately contrived peepholes allow the women to have a one-way view of any visitors.
Outdoors, the **ruag** of the tent is replaced by the mask - **burga** - worn by females from the age of seven.

Absorbed in the explanation of the weaver who reveals to us... the finer points of her craft, we do not notice the sleek silhouette of a saluki* standing as if out of a medieval engraving. Inside

---

* saluki - desert greyhound

The pulley squeaks on its axle. Diriyah oasis in the Najd. (p. 42)

When inner tubes become water tubes. (p.43)

Reduced to a parcel of meat : the dromedary. Najran souk.

Perennial interaction at the Najran souk. (p.46)

Local craft work is flourishing and meets essential needs. (p.47)

the tent, he enjoys the same standing as the falcon. For the Bedouin, these two hunting companions are - like the telephone in Saudian automobiles - an indication of social status. Like man, the saluki has porous skin that breathes - differentiating it from the rest of the canine race.

Any unexpected distraction is a godsend. A neighbour calls in, greets her friend, and offers her hand to Danielle and lifts it to her lips. I offer my hand but she only brushes the tips of my fingers reluctantly. She sits down near to my wife and starts to work a few tufts of goat-hair on a spindle and distaff - **mighzal** and **mighzala**. Between her fingers, the yarn twists and untwists. Skill in handling even the most simple tools often requires long practice. Danielle tries her hand at carding, spinning and weaving - activities traditionally practiced only by women - and quickly picks up the gist. The spinner stops working for a moment to touch Danielle's hair, fascinated by its colour. She examines her gently but thoroughly, trying to find evidence of a possible pregnancy.

Our hostess asks the name of our tribe, to which I reply "Faransa". France is too far away and I am not understood.

The noise of a car interrupts this intimate discussion. It is the woman's husband, alerted by a mysterious "bush telegraph". He greets me, paying no attention to Danielle, as any gesture towards her would be considered offensive. We gather round the hearth, just a hole in the ground, surrounded by familiar objects - a cooking pot mounted on a tripod, gracefully curved coffee pots, a frequently used teapot, the bread platter used as a windbreak, ornate coffee spoon, poker and the ever-present mortar.

A soothing light filters through the goat-hair roof. The desert has become bearable under the tent's micro-climate. As a prelude to Bedouin hospitality, we are settled down on a plastic mat - a material that certainly was not around in Abraham's time. A few cheeky young goats wander over leaving a trail of droppings in their wake and fix us with their insolent stares. They poke their noses everywhere, tails swishing like metronomes, sniffing at leftovers and licking plates. A young girl rises and graciously ushers them out.

Our host's joviality gives way to the serious business of preparing coffee. With the ease that comes from long practice, he fans the dying cinders back into life with the bottom of his robe -**thowb**. While waiting for the water to boil, he roasts some coffee beans in the iron **mihmas**, turning them with a spatula until ready. He then crushes them to a fine powder in the **nigr**, a bronze mortar which is virtually a large upturned bell that rings when struck on its rim or base. Depending on how it is held, a variety of sounds can be produced. Lulled by the beat, we sit around the hearth dreaming of another, more primitive way of life, of which we only have confused notions. The fire gives free rein to our thoughts, occupying the eye but not the mind. Perhaps this encounter with our ancient cousins the Bedouins has stirred up long-dormant feelings ?

The man tips powdered coffee into the pot - **della** - then brings it to the boil a second time. While waiting, he crushes some cardamon - the Bedouins believe it has aphrodisiacal properties - tosses it into the water and boils it once again. Some add an homeopathic dose of ginger or saffron - always specially

A diabolical glint in a Bedouin's eye.

The half-mask contributes to feminine appeal. Waghla in Najran. (p. 50)

Artificial colorants have added greater diversity to the range of colours. (p. 51)

A Yam woman composes a colour symphony on the strings of her silent instrument. Rub Al Khali. (p. 51)

prepared each time - the quality of the ingredients, the dosage and the host's knowledge being essential to the process.

He places a palm-fibre filter over the spout of the pot then brings out some cups without handles from the **shait** - a box made from copper. He burns incense - **bakhur** - in a tiny iron dish -**fels** - over which he inverts each cup before stacking them in his right hand. The spout plunges into the first cup and is then drawn confidently upwards, the height of the gesture measuring the amount poured - a short coffee, savoured like a liqueur.

Custom requires that at least three cups be drunk - the first with surprise, the second with a smirk and the third with gratified triumph at the success of the brew. Only the right hand must be used to drink, and there are no exceptions for left handers. Having no wish to upset our host, we abide to the rules. According to Michel Tournier, the right hand is "the most spiritual part of the body, that which produces calligraphy - the algebra of the soul". The left hand is considered impure - the hand that is used for cleaning after relieving oneself.

The soothing coffee "ritual", with its calculated slowness, helps to soften the hardship of desert life. Under this tent belonging to another era, life moves at the same rhythm as the desert ; everything - despite the somewhat anachronistic watch worn by our host - contributing to strip time of its substance.

There is a year-round time lag between our time system and theirs. It prevails right across the Peninsula and in accordance with the setting of the sun.

Whilst the wife is giving her husband a detailed account of our every word and deed since arriving, young girls pass to and fro in front of the **majlis** - furtive shadows accompanied by the rustling of dresses and tinkling of jewelry. Doubtlessly, the presence of strangers is the event of the day.

I am as curious as they are. My attention was initially drawn to traditional objects, but now I start noticing things such as a suitcase, a transistorized radio, a porta-gas cooker and aluminium utensils. Unremarkable in appearance, they create a breach opening up the flood-gates to another culture. Although the black tent remains an ever-familiar sight in the desert landscape, when crossed with modernism it becomes something quite surreal. It is clear however that these early signs of western influence arouse more interest from a sociological than an artistic point of view. Bedouins are infected with the modernism that is inherent to civilization ; in accepting the excesses of an "oil-drenched" country, they progressively lose control over their destiny and subsequently lose their identity. They are gradually contracting a marriage of convenience and as a recompense for their submission receive a dowry of comfort and security. Without a worthwhile fight, will they not gradually become impotent ? In spite of all this, must they loose their soul ?

T.E. Lawrence described nomadic lifestyle as "the vital flux that gives the Semitic body its vigour". It is tempting to suggest that the Bedouin of tomorrow will be as different from the Bedouin of yesterday as the feral cat is different from its domesticated cousin. Since hydrocarbons have been mined in the country, a great many Bedouins have been absorbed into the oil industry. One of the most rugged human adventures is coming to an end on the oil rigs.

Purity in two words : sand and wind.

The pride of a Yam meharist... Rub al Khali. (p.54)

Dahm encampment asleep for eternity in the oppressive heat of the day. Rub al Khali.(p.55)

In keeping with warrior tradition, many have joined the army. The fact is, many young Bedouins prefer the rigours of military life to the uncertainties of pastoral nomadism. One of them pointed out to me, quite pertinently, that the people who love the desert are not necessarily those who live in it.

We are not too foolish to realize that it is only possible to begin to know a people by sharing their life and hardships over long periods.

In the meantime we can nevertheless sample the charm of their customs. After enjoying the coffee we drink tea with a somewhat goaty flavour that comes from the water-skin, **guerba**. Bringing the ceremonial to an end, our host generously splashes perfume on our heads and hands - the most flattering gesture of desert hospitality.

The ruthless midday sun beats down on the landscape, washing out the colour. Our host retires to pray. In the silence and purity of this vast landscape, we sense a divine presence. Five times a day, the sand unfurls its immense prayer mat for Allah's shepherd to kneel on. In this arid land, sand is used as a symbolic alternative to water for ablutions. When prayers have ended, the faithful remain kneeling in long meditation before returning to reality.

The younger women have been eagerly waiting for the right moment to meet with Danielle. A young girl is sent ahead as a scout, then under the host's apparently indifferent eye, they sneak their way into the **majilis**. Their curiosity sweeps away the usual restraints and reserve. We greet the most senior

woman. Her life's journey has engraved many lines on her face. In the ancient manner, she wears the **khayt** - goathair coiled on her head like a bird's nest. Seven silver rings, set off by coral-coloured fingernails, brighten up her dark clothes. The half-mask - **al miltham** - with its tinkling chains, covers the lower part of her face. The wide sleeves of her robe touch the ground. Around her waist is a plaited leather belt from which hangs a heavy and ancient key.

Her half-mask is continuously slipping down. There is an often repeated male joke at the expense of the old women ; "They have eaten so many old nanny-goats that they have lost their teeth !" The stick of **rak,** which they carry with them at all times, contradicts gossip-mongers. **Rak**, the fibrous root of the Miswak tree, contains an antiseptic and it is used as a natural toothbrush.

Perhaps, in this land of masks, beauty needs to be considered in a different way. Nowhere do a woman's eyes reveal so much of her feelings. Her large **khol**-rimmed eyes spark off fires fanned by the desert wind !

For the Saudis - although unable to see behind these masks - the eyes tell of the woman's beauty. Large black eyes are referred to as woman's most important attribute and grace the **houris**, the heavenly virgins promised by Allah to his faithful on entering Paradise.

For many westerners, the masked woman is still the symbol of Moslem society. The protective screen of the mask guards women against prying male eyes and wind-blown sand that irritates the face and dries out lips. It only takes a short stay in the desert to realize the necessity of this mask and of the **ghutra**, the head cover worn by Saudi men.

Yam elder prepares coffee with age-old gestures. Rub al Khali.

Not quite the usual sparse Bedouin-style furnishings ! Shammar of the Nafud.

56

On the women's foreheads dark marks suggest the presence of **washam** - tatoos. In the intimacy of the women's section, Danielle has discovered that most of them are adorned with dots and vertical lines tattooed with acacia needles impregnated with charcoal from the fires.

Rather than using pockets, the women hang various objects from their shawls - keys, tweezers for extracting thorns and, occasionally, a magnificent silver triangle, punctuated by a red stone. They are staggered to see that Danielle is not wearing jewelry. Should not every husband lavishly adorn his wife ? Nomad women attach a great deal of importance to jewelry which becomes their permanent property after marriage and their sole means of hoarding wealth.

Nowadays, Bedouin women sell off their traditional jewelry to antique dealers and buy up recently-made gold items.

Many of the women carry the **hirz** - a silver tube containing verses from the Koran or perfumed pieces of cloth. As do many other traditional objects, the **hirz** displays the signs of a rich occult symbolism.

The women are fascinated and eagerly bombard Danielle with questions. They are surprised and disquieted by the answers. They are all ears when Danielle explains why western couples have so few children. The more embarrassing details bring on peals of laughter accompanied by hand-claps and a rising crescendo of "yooo". Danielle allows her handbag to be subjected to a detailed inspection by the women who discover all the little accessories that women use.

Danielle's white feet provoke a great deal of interest whilst her long fingernails attract reproving looks.

She notices that most of the children are terrified when I look at them through my sunglasses. I remove them and my blue eyes provoke the same effect as Danielle's feet.

During this time our host has slaughtered a goat. The animal was laid on its side with its head towards Mecca and the name of Allah -**bismilla** - is invoked. The animal jerks, blood runs into the sand. One last spasm and the beast is still. The head is impaled on a stick, browned over the flames, then placed in the cooking pot. A young Bedouin empties the intestines by pressing them between his fingers. He washes and grills them and is soon enjoying this delicacy. I ask if I can visit the women in their quarters. Inside it is utter chaos. In the centre of the room is a miraculously preserved **tama** - the bedding once lashed onto the dromedary's back to carry women and children on the long migratory treks. It is constructed from wood and sacking and now is part of a boudoir. It was not long ago -perhaps fifteen years - that it was mounted on camels. The scene is still alive in my mind, a romantic image handed down by XIXth century orientalists and explorers.

This "gondola" would have had much the same soothing effect as a rocking-chair, which, for sensitive stomachs could bring on sickness. This was due to the constant pitching and tossing of the dromedary whose flanks move in unison. This provides at least one explanation for the dromedary's title of "ship of the desert"...

"Grazing by night, the voices of our camels are like the rolling, growling thunder of dawn.

Ship of the desert, those you carry are safe. And how much greater the risk on board a ship of the sea !"

A pick-up truck, totally out of place,

For the Bedouins, hospitality has become a cardinal virtue. Shammar of the Nafud.

occupies the third compartment of the tent. The automobile plays a significant role in the Bedouin's daily life. The present does not cancel out the past and the bedding alongside the pick-up is yet another indicator of the prevailing confusion. The pragmatic Bedouins are always prepared to quickly change their methods for more practical alternatives. Nomads do not become attached to many things - their laws only permit them to own as much as can be carried by the dromedary. The real wealth of the Bedouin - their age-old knowledge - is carried within.

Further on, tents made from white tarpaulin fill the gaps between scattered traditional tents. These tarpaulins first appeared on the country's reconstruction sites and, judging by their widespread acceptance, could very well take over completely from the black tents. To retain the traditional lay out of the original black tent, each one of its compartments would have to be replaced by a white tent, consequently altering the configuration of the camp. The Bedouins would prefer to retain the concept of the **ruag**, although it has lost its original function. The technique, however, is now restricted to embroidery of naive floral motifs.

In adopting the new look, these tents lost their rustic accoutrements, which have been replaced by flashy - often plastic - imports. All that was essential to this civilization is disappearing, giving way to by-products of the oil industry. Bedouins cannot comprehend the value that we attach to these old objects once owned by their ancestors. The left-overs of modern technology, such as tyres and inner-tubes, are recycled to produce buckets, sandals and water containers. However, despite the use of different materials,

design concepts have not radically changed.

Whilst we visited the camp, our hostess has been putting final touches to the meal. We all gather around a platter, piled high with rice and goat meat. According to the laws of sharing, eating together puts a seal on our friendship.
Although Bedouins live with extremely restricted means, their generosity knows no bounds and it helps to maintain social prestige. To safeguard his reputation, the chief of a tribe keeps open table ; inside his tent the sound of the mortar and pestle can be heard from dawn to dusk - a sure sign of food being prepared.

Men and women eat separately - masculine dignity does not allow otherwise. After asking Allah's blessing, right sleeves are rolled up and hands dive into the rice and goat meat dish - **kebsa**. The meal is simple but delicious and abundant. Handfuls of rice are pressed in the palm, rolled into a ball and popped into the mouth. Acting as a fork, fingers of the right hand break up the meat. The host selects the tastiest morsels and tosses them graciously onto the guest's portion. The well-picked gleaming bones are placed in a small pile before the eater, who belches when finished then wipes his mouth with the back of his hand and leaves the table to wash his hands under a fine trickle of water, poured from a jug by the host. Soap-powder has taken the place of sand for washing, in preference to soap which lacks sand's abrasive quality. In the old days, it was quite normal to wipe greasy fingers on the beard or on part of the tent wall, where many stains reflected the hospitality of the host. These days, he offers you a towel...

"Let peace be with you"

60

Sand is used to scour the platter. It has other uses ; at any given moment, a Bedouin is likely to squat down, in what appears to be pious meditation and - well concealed by his **thowb** - relieve himself in public. A Westerner, wearing trousers, does not have the same resources and must wait for nightfall or the early hours to find a relatively isolated spot.

Now that we are accepted and part of the village life, we can move freely around the tents. Visiting the camp makes us even more aware of the surrounding void. A solitary Bedouin rider looms up out of the shimmering heat of the dunes.
Reb Safad says "The desert prompts a nostalgia for the sea". This civilization is quintessentially represented by the partnership of man and animal - a mythical encounter forever linked to the desert landscape. Bedouins venerate the dromedary and see it as the symbol of their identity.
According to Van Hammer Pungstall, 5,744 names and epithets refer to the Arabian camel. It was through its domestication - which occurred some four thousand years along the southern edge of the Rub al Khali - that the Bedouins found their supremacy. This animal's mobility and endurance gave the Bedouin cameleers - the tent dwelling nomads - great power over those who only owned goats or sheep. Nowadays - as well as camels - the Bedouins raise goats and sheep. Their movements have been relatively restricted by the sheep - the animal least adapted to desert conditions. Now their lifestyle is smoothly progressing towards semi-nomadism before taking the irreversible step of sedenterization.

The meharist, rocked by the ambling gait of his mount, stops in front of us.

He nimbly dismounts and brings the animal, bleating reluctantly, to its knees. Without her master's approval she is impossible to approach and jerks back her head violently like "an outraged old duchess". Nonetheless, I give it a try. With a gnashing of yellow teeth, she grumbles her discontent in great raucous gurgles. Her master strokes her muzzle to calm her down a little. On the animal's neck can be seen the **wasm** - a furrowed scar, applied with a red-hot iron to identify her lineage, a combination of single and juxtaposed geometric symbols.

The cameleer, with his enormous cartridge-belt, looks like a raider out of a Thesiger odyssey. He sports a **khanjar**, the nomad dagger and an imposing rifle left over from the Yemen war. There is only one thing missing - my binoculars, which he eyes covetously ! Then and there, I hand them over. Delighted with his acquisition, he climbs a dune and scans the horizon for his herd. Binoculars give them the eye of a falcon and are particularly appreciated. Musil mentions how certain people, in order to improve their range of sight, smear kohl around the edges of their lenses.
When our hostess sees what I have done, she goes to a chest and takes out a magnificent plaited leather belt, similar to those worn by the Yam women. She winds it - all five metres of it - around Danielle's waist. The fewer the number of turns, the more the jibes...

The setting sun sits atop a dune. A woolly regiment of fat-tailed sheep drag themselves across the sand. A few goats rush down the slope and push their way through the crowd to the troughs: Returning from prayers, our host swings the **madkhana**, a perfumeburner, in front of us. The last image

62

of the day, seen through a perfumed halo, will remain for us, a slow, majestic procession of dromedaries - a distant echo of the spice-laden caravans of another era.

Although stripped of their harness and noble charge, the camels of Arabia have lost none of their magnificence. They come to quench their thirst from the **hawd** - the huge drinking-skins. They drink feverishly, their long necks curved like birds in flight. Their capacity to absorb water matches their legendary sobriety and once they have drunk plentifully - up to one hundred litres of water, a quarter of their own weight ! - they lick greedily on large salt blocks, making enormous craters with their rasping tongues. Curly-haired baby camels leap friskily around their re-found mothers. The men remove their weaning halters, the **shmala**. Once they have drunk their fill of the abundantly flowing milk, the men pull them off to fill their own bowls. These are passed from hand to hand, each person taking a long draught, leaving frothy mustaches. Our turn has come. As I detest milk, Danielle drinks for two, which is something of a shock and an offence to our friends. It is true that camel milk, rich in vitamin C, is the basis of their diet.

A milking camel can produce four litres of milk every day for eleven months after she has given birth. It is said that a female's hump is sometimes too large and her mate's genitals too small for her to be mounted without assistance from the master. We are told an Arab version of this story ; Noah ordered all male animals to leave their virile attributes on the gangplank before entering the ark. When they disembarked, they all retrieved their property, except for the dromedary who, last to leave, could only find the donkey's.

Men hobble their dromedaries to restrict their wandering habits.

The herdswomen are put to the test in this mass of hooves and horns, doing their utmost to bring about some semblance of order. Moving between goats and ewes, they draw off the milk. Later, the young animals are individually tethered to a line stretched between two stakes.

A Bedouin woman who was with her herd all afternoon, joins us under the tent. A cloth covered leather cot is slung over her shoulder. She never leaves her child - the two live at the same rhythm. When older and out of his leather chrysalis, the child will start to get curious and sometimes put himself in danger.

For this reason, and to restrict the range of children's activity, they are tied up to a tent-post. This substitute for an umbilical cord lessens the risk of a fall into the fire !

The rumbling of camels, the sounds of swallowing and the plaintive bleating of livestock are dying down.

The fire lights up the tent - just enough for the Bedouins to go about the final activities of the day.

We take advantage of the last glow of twilight to put up our tent, positioned at a respectable distance from the camp to avoid any interference from insomniac camels. They have already checked out the trunk of the car and left moist and sandy trails with their dribbling muzzles. After clearing a space amongst the droppings, we unfold the tent and erect it, not without attracting attention. Everyone is extremely interested and they study the process carefully. They have never seen a tent like it ! The divider between lobby and sleeping compartment suggests their rule of separation - but this

After the meal...

64

is where the comparison ends. A child hammers in the tent-pegs with a pestle. Some of the less timorous women summon up enough courage to venture inside. Wide-eyed, they inspect the different sections. The cramped sleeping compartment, suggesting a certain intimacy, brings on mischievous smiles.

We gather around the fireplace for coffee in the solemn presence of the patriarch. He rules with the wisdom acquired over long years. A baby snuggles up to her mother's breast and feeds with determination. According to the precepts of Islamic morality, it is totally acceptable for women to exhibit themselves whilst feeding a child. Fertility is considered woman's cardinal virtue and explains why most Bedouin women are either pregnant or nursing. The young boy serving us is not sure to whom he should give the first cup ; his father takes it and, without hesitation, hands it to the patriarch, thereby confirming the eternal hierarchy that comes with age. The few cups are passed from one person to the other, each drinking a mouthful with delight. At the slightest sign, our young waiter is ready to refill the cups.
"Our constant fire glows brightly, beckoning the night visitor. It gives sustenance, assuaging cold and hunger".

We are somewhere between heaven and earth, slipping back to a more simple, primitive existence. We feel that we are experiencing something unique. Capricious flames cast a flickering glow on faces, setting off jewelry and masks, catching the flash of gold teeth. They love to spend time talking. The men enjoy launching into lengthy tirades, however mundane they may be. A good talker gains standing and acceptance. Women, who keep their thoughts to themselves during the day, open up at night. A theatrical performance is put on for us and we have no trouble in following every detail. Like Lamartine, we are able to follow discussion through "the sound of the voice, facial expression, the shuddering of the listeners".

We have a quick and simple meal of bread dipped in milk. The long discussions start up again. Our overnight companions explain with concern that they have been waiting four years for the drought to break and the vegetation to flourish again. A Bedouin raises his open hand upwards indicating that all is dependent on Allah's will.
Wilfred Thesiger wrote : "a cloud forms, rain falls, men live ; the cloud disperses, no more rain, men and animals die".

There is no rebellion in the speaker's expression, only tremendous resignation - the very essence of Islam. For the Bedouins rain is a God-sent gift. In the meantime they have to bring fodder from Najran and face the possibility of a prolonged drought.

Amongst us there is a **Najrani** who is here a weekend with his family, thus experiencing both urban and Bedouin life styles. I show him my Temporary Residence Visa. In Arabia, this indispensible document is testimony to a man's honesty. He reads through it attentively. Reassured, he helps us to write down the dialect names of various objects around the tent. He uses a part of his **thowb** as a rest to write on. To everybody's amazement, he continues our dialogue in English - displaying the Saudi gift for language, cultivated either abroad or in their contact with foreigners.
We show them our book, "A l'ombre

Five prayers punctuate the Bedouins' day.

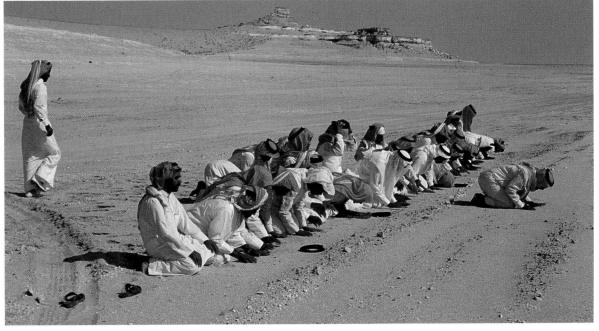

des tentes noires" , a title which conveys the feeling we wanted to impart of precious moments spent with these people. They look through the book selectively, showing no interest whatsoever in unfamiliar worlds, whereas any photo which relates to them provokes lengthy commentary. The images awaken sleeping memories and they recount tales of their joys and sufferings. As for the women, they actually kiss the photographs of children. For the elders, seeing Thomas J. Abercrombie's shots from **National Geographic** is like watching a movie of their own past.

Shots of a dromedary caravan with mounted bedding arouse even more excitement, bringing back memories of the long migratory treks. An old woman, rocking back and forth, intones an ancient chant. The harsh reality of Bedouin life is a continuous cloud of melancholy. The images speak of a disappearing world that will soon only belong in the country's collective unconscious.

The patriarch, filled with memories of a heroic age, strokes his chin. It is as though a long forgotten existence was being relived in his mind with a burning desire to pick up where he left off. We suspect that he is dreaming of the old razzias. These raids, which involved attacking camps, seizing goods and livestock, were considered a noble and manly institution. In order to avoid vendettas, the aggressors did not take life. The razzia was a way to redistribute wealth acting as a control mechanism. Such plundering was a means of achieving glory and a way to feed the legends of the Peninsula. Then the poets sang the praises of the glorious men in their verses which, to maintain tribal prestige, were passed down through the generations. The days of the razzias are over. When the King-

dom was established, Ibn Saoud put an end to these practices. We have met these Bedouins, warriors without arms, peacefully tending their herds.

They are not concerned about theft, implicitly protected by their cohesion and its in-built surveillance system. Only the women's coffers are padlocked.

Between sips, one of the men is fiddling with his feet. Nothing to be shocked about - the sand keeps them perfectly clean. Another one "works" his gums with a stick of **rak**. The patriarch strokes his marbled beard. Absent-mindedly, their hands tell the ninety-nine beads of the **misbaha**. We speculate on the age of the grandfather who everybody likes to think is a hundred years old, a universal preference for this number.

Sometimes we catch glimpses of a face when masks are surreptitiously lifted to drink. The younger girls go through the motions of hastily concealing this impropriety, but never miss a sly glance to check its effect.

A perfume-burner is passed around to avert the evil eye and get rid of disagreeable smells. Each person catches a little of the smoke with a wide sweep of their hand and savours it under their headcover.

The patriarch slowly heaves himself up onto his large calloused feet with the aid of a knobbly stick. The noise dies down ; conversation stops and only a few murmurs mixed with an occasional bleat can be heard. The baby is fast asleep, still clinging to his mother's breast.

A woman throws sand on the fire to put it out. She is dropping the tent's side-wall as we leave.

The moon floats over the large black tents.

The last prayer of the day. After their ablutions, the men kneel, elbow to elbow, behind a line traced in the sand - **masjid** - representing the mosque. They bow and kneel in perfect synchrony. When the chanting finishes, the men return to their tents, each with a small patch of sand on their forehead - some of the more ardent devotees have even developed a hard lump. They roll themselves into their rugs and fall asleep, worn out by the long chatter. For them, there are no sleepless nights or air-conditioned nightmares.

The stars are beautiful, bright and numerous as always. The sky, like a mirror, seems to be reflecting the lights of the camp a thousand times over.
The Milky Way hangs out its glimmering scarf across the sky. Arabs like to believe that it comes from a trail of blood from the celestial ram sent to Abraham when, obeying God's command, he raised his knife to sacrifice his son. A legend worthy of the decor !

Morning prayer call challenges the sleepers as the clear pale light of dawn slips into our tent. The beautiful chanting, heard so many times before at first light, never fails in its mystical impact.

Sunrise is greeted by children's coughs and the noise of the animals. Imagine our surprise at finding a bowl of frothing milk waiting for us outside our tent ! Hospitality being contagious, we offer them some coffee which is either refused or reluctantly tasted and then spat out. The Bedouins eat a very limited range of food and find it hard to cope with new taste experiences.

The morning wash is not much more than a splash ; water, being so precious, is saved for more important use.

The animals are set free and they race to the feeding troughs, a few horns getting hooked up en route. A formidable looking billy with lyre-shaped horns discourages the more impetuous amongst them.
A few pebbles thrown at them soon sorts them into lines at the trough. Women bring back bowls overflowing with frothy milk.

Reptiles and other nocturnal creatures have left their signatures on the naked dunes. One in particular suggests that its author is still around...
Intrigued, we watch a man checking the surrounds of our tent. He follows a track in the sand as far as a shrub, then stops. Suddenly, he slams the stick down. A snake is lying twisting and writhing on the ground. A sand viper had decided to make its home under our ground sheet !
Bedouins always follow the same procedure for snake-bites - they are sucked, cut and removed after being cauterized with boiling butter.

Everybody stokes their fires. Smoke rises from the tents and the dull, regular sound of a butter churn can be heard. A goatskin bag - semila - is being shaken in regular swinging movements by one of the women, turning cream into butter.
Mortars and pestles are busy.
Early in the fresh of dawn, three generations have taken their place around the fire. Snuggled under their blankets, sleepy children rub their eyes. The patriarch wears a heavy camel skin coat - **mishla** - over his shoulders. Coffee pots gleam in the rising sun. We drink ginger-flavoured goatsmilk, tea and coffee into which we dip our dates.

Reminder of a warrior past. A Dahm tribesman

Camel racing and the falcon hunt are traditional activities of the Al Murrah Bedouins from Ambak. (p. 73)

70

Before the goats decide to make it their latest playground, we pack our tent. The sterility of the environment makes the goatshair tent a particularly attractive home. The surrounding emptiness turns it into a rather special luxury.

As the dromedaries are given plenty of freedom, the herdsman's role is reduced to pointing them in the right direction and letting them wander off. The ocean of sand quickly swallows them up. They travel six miles or so before returning at sunset. Their entire life is spent scraping a meagre pittance from the sand.

Goats and sheep pour out of the encampment. Young shepherds carry a few dates and some bread in a small bag, enough food for the day. The livestock continue their tireless quest. Month after month, year after year, with no other goal but to seek out food for their survival... and in turn to provide food for their masters.

Once the herds have gone a kind of apathy descends on the camp. Only women and children remain. The menfolk seem to have disappeared. When we might have thought that they were simply taking pleasurable strolls they are, in fact, continually on the rove, carrying out various tasks: checking new grazing ground, maintaining contact with neighbours, inspecting the livestock, dealing in the souk, replenishing water supplies.

The desert is crisscrossed by a network of interconnecting paths. But beware of "secondary" tracks - they are there to get you lost...

As the sun gets higher, the ground gets warmer. The women meet in tents and relax. Nora, who has become Danielle's confidante, delights in dressing her up in tribal costume. She spends hours winding on the goatshair head dress, providing a source of great amusement for the women.

Still overwhelmed by the warmth of our reception we prepare to go our way. Women let down a corner of their masks, just enough to be able to kiss Danielle. Nora deftly slips a gold ring onto one of her fingers. Spontaneously, Danielle offers Nora one of her rings. Often, during our prolonged and close contact with nomads, a mutual affection has developed between Danielle and one of her hostesses, usually affirmed by the exchange of gifts, rings in particular.

Before starting the car, I drag out a few goats sprawling underneath.

Over the years we try and keep in touch with our friends - although not without difficulty. We, sometimes, just by chance, find them at the end of a long journey.

There is something sad about their perpetual movement, their constant comings and goings and precarious living arrangements. Ancestral customs have given the Bedouins an extraordinary capacity to construct and organize the goatshair tents. During the first year I spent in Saudi Arabia, I made a fool of myself, being totally unaware that men never get involved in this work. And my goodness, how the women laughed !

Every time a camp is set up a new track is created and another is forgotten. Bedouins always leave behind an assorted medley of discarded objects, a superfluous load jettisoned before leaving stopovers.

The scattered left-overs of two intermingling cultures evoke the beginnings

Does he know, this young Al Murrah, the absolute beauty of the desert ? (p. 74)

The erg, an ocean of sand stilled for eternity (p. 75)

76

of a rubbish dump; discarded hides, empty cans, bones, broken glass, dismembered carcasses of animals, bits of old tyres, heads and legs of goats. On a carpet of animal droppings, the tents have left patches of unsullied ground. Just so many traces that tell of the camp's fleeting and turbulent existence. Long before the nomads were aware of consumer society waste, the elegies of Pre-Islamic Arab poets - Umru al Qays, Tarafa, Antara, Labid - had captured the sadness of abandoned encampments.

The desert unfolds its dunes at the pace of the dromedary as it has done for time immemorial. Rub al Khali.

The portable drinking trough of the Al Murrah from the Rub al Khali. (p. 82)

An Atawi elder watches the sea of sand die at his feet (p. 83)

Among the Dahm Bedouins.

The tents, traces of charcoal on a golden page, fade into the distance and vanish into the horizon. Great tongues of sand come to lick the road. We are approaching a police checkpoint close by a beautiful black tent festooned with electric light bulbs.

The same decor...but with different lighting. The tent of the sedentary Bedouin serves a persistent nomadic yearning. Even though they have settled, they perpetuate the rituals of the desert.

Inside the police post, we sit down in the **majlis.** The police wear flamboyant cartridge belts across their chests and fierce looking rifles complete the scene. One of the policemen is playing with a **dhab**, an antediluvian lizard with short, powerful legs, sharp claws and a tail covered with formidable spikes. The animal will keep him company until it is big enough to eat. We are surprised to see another of the men wearing his hair in two long curls that frame his face - a style that was popular several decades ago but rarely seen these days.

While the men are serving us coffee and dates, the Emir - apparently not surprised to see us - greets us affably. He must have known that two strangers with a strange passion for old objects have been visiting the encampments over the past few days. In keeping with good manners, he does not question us. It is not done to ask an unexpected visitor the reason for his visit. Respecting Arab psychology we play the waiting game, withholding the essential and approaching it through more subtle and devious ways. The next step of our voyage could well depend on this relationship. The authorities, unable to guarantee a visitor's safety, generally prefer to prevent

entry into this border zone, the subject of a dispute with a rather worrying neighbour : South Yemen.

We eventually reveal our passion for the Bedouin people and ask the Emir if we may visit the tent. He doesn't seem to understand. We are staggered to see this elderly man pulling on a hair of his beard to make sure we are both talking about the same thing ! Then he grabs my hand and leads us to the tent.
After the visit, the Emir checks my papers. Once again my card from the Ministry of Defense and Aviation stands me in good stead. He calls over a policeman and places him at our disposal - an offer difficult to refuse.

Escorted by the policeman in his "GMC" mounted with a machine-gun, we are approaching a Dahm encampment. These Bedouins live on the southern edge of the Rub al Khali and skip freely from Yemen to Saudi Arabia. A crowd with small bushy heads and runny noses forms our reception committee. Within seconds, the women disappear from view. The chief is rather disquieted at the sight of two Westerners escorted by a policeman. He adjusts his turban, his cartridge belt and his dagger and offers his greetings, looking us straight in the eyes. We are invited into the tent. An ancient rifle hangs from a tent-post, like a corporate sign, a reminder that the Bedouins have not disarmed.
The sound of giggles and animated chatter can be heard from the women's quarters where Danielle has just arrived. When separation of the sexes is the order of the day, as is the case here, Danielle spends most of her time with the women but has the very special privilege of moving freely between the **majlis** and the women's compartment. Although the elders remain stolidly in-

The "ruag" separates the men's quarters from the women's. Al Murrah from the Rub al Khali. (p. 84-85)

In the women's quarter : A palanquin of the Yam from the Rub al Khali.

different, the sight of an outsider arouses the young men's dormant energy who nevertheless put on an air of detachment...

Our host prepares coffee. This "ritual" of calculated slowness gives him an opportunity to look over his guests and to sound out their intentions. Are we on an official mission ?
"**Qahwa** !" he grumbles authoritatively towards the women concealed behind the **ruag**.
From behind the **ruag** a furtive hand holds out a bag of coffee.

The sound of the pestle attracts people from all over the camp. Several men, attracted by the coffee - and by our presence - come over and we greet them, the usual polite formulas springing forth automatically. On entering the tent they remove their sandals.
We are impressed by their military bearing and distinguished appearance. They each carry a silver dagger in their belts. Most Bedouins would like to carry a modern weapon, either a pistol or a Kalachnikov, smuggled in from Yemen. Even though the razzia has seen its day, the warrior spirit still lives on. Not forgetting that a visitor is much more favourably judged if he has a knowledge of firearms, I spend a few moments sharing their passion for the rifles they proudly show me.
Each time a new visitor arrives, glasses are topped up once more - the hours could be counted by the amount of tea drunk. The aroma of mint from the tea fills the room. It is savoured with great delight.

Danielle tells them she is a nurse and immediately a man shows her his hands covered with eczema. These people who prefer to submit their health problems to an apparently competent visitor rather than to anonymous dispensary personnel, place themselves entirely in Danielle's hands. Some of them present her with simple scratches, just to watch her in action.
A few patients sit around her and await their turn. One man's knee is swollen from a rheumatic node. Danielle sighs, aware of her impotence...

The days spent practicing medical care were not all quite so calm. In one of the camps, an anxious father is tending his sick child. Danielle gives the child aspirin to reduce his temperature but ten minutes later he is in convulsions. Panic-stricken, the father starts screaming, takes the child and drives him twelve miles to the dispensary. Danielle is feeling somewhat responsible as we wait a good five hours at the camp to hear finally that the child was suffering from sunstroke. Imagine the consequences had he not survived !
In this particular case, we cannot underestimate the possibility of blood vengeance being taken during the three days that follow the "crime".

These days, the law of "an eye for an eye and a tooth for a tooth" has been replaced by cash payments for loss of life. This is the price for blood ; the families of the, unfortunately all too frequent, fatal road accident victims, are entitled to a compensation of around $35,000.

Elsewhere, we have witnessed the common Bedouin practice of ignipuncture. Western doctors are often amazed to see burns - from a practice not unlike blood letting - on the affected area of the skin. An elderly woman complains of violent head pain ; to the Bedouin healer's disapproval, Danielle gives her a tablet. The **mekwa** - an iron rod - is made red-hot on a bed of coals. He ap-

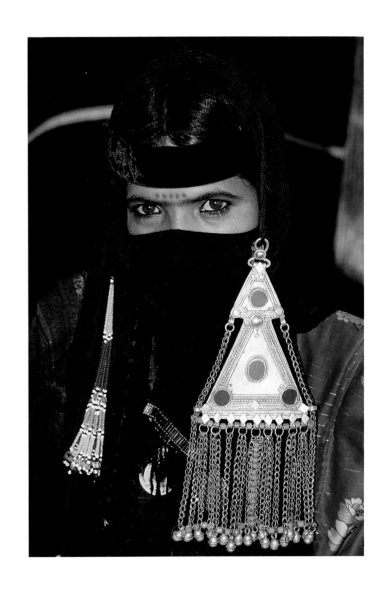

plies it to two specific points on the top of the head.

Added to the suffering of the woman, the smell of burning flesh is terrible to bear. No doubt the healing will be attributed to the iron rods !

Bloated with tea and their curiosity satisfied, the men rise one after another, put on their shoes, take their guns and leave the tent without as much as a glimpse toward the host. Such is the custom...

When the visitors have left, a young girl squats down and starts to prepare dough which is then placed over the fire on a **saj**. She puts out a bowl of clarified butter, which – so our male Bedouin friends tell us – greatly improves virility ! Our being childless is a source of great mystery for everybody and although they would dearly love to know why, they can only guess... To save face, Danielle invents a daughter, at school in France, a half-truth since we are talking about my daughter.

The man boasts that he has two wives - a fact that brags of both his virility and prestige - polygamy being a very expensive practice. He takes great pleasure in emphasizing the size of his family, carefully listing every one of his children. More through politeness than conviction, we congratulate him.

Everyone gathers around the bowl of golden liquid and the bread that the young girl has just taken from the fire. Taking a piece of bread in their right hands, they knead it into a scoop and vying with each other, dip it into the melted butter. After using the piece two or three times, they swallow it and make a new one.

Our host, noticing that we are only taking tiny nibbles, courteously insists that we do justice to the dish. Our stomachs are not nearly as curious as our minds. Paradoxically, Bedouins eat only a small amount of meat. The killing of animals - which diminishes their stock and thus, their capital - is reserved for very special occasions.

Caught up in this whirlwind of conviviality, we are given very little choice. Any attempt to put off an invitation to eat is either doomed to failure or runs the risk of seriously offending our hosts.

This evening I am stuck in bed with a heavy bout of amoebic dysentery. Danielle has been left to cope with the conversation on her own. She has managed - diplomatically - to send the policeman back to his base. Tomorrow, we leave without a chaperon.

Objective - Sharora.

A pick-up truck has fallen victim to the treacherous sands and is buried down to its axle, heaving up the ground, its wheels spinning. Carrying a huge load of camp equipment, it seems to defy the laws of gravity. A Bedouin is clearing large amounts of sand from under the wheels - Long Live the Dromedary ! ! ! We tow out the vehicle and the driver thanks us profusely. Maybe he will do the same for us one day !

We head back onto the undulating road. After a short distance we start to bounce over a series of humps coming up to a road-block, manned by a dozing policeman. He is somewhat reticent to let us pass and subjects us to a thorough interrogation. He is puzzled by our presence and wonders why we are interested in the desert. We go through the motions of a dialogue. My papers, signed and countersigned, finally convince him that he should let us proceed. He lifts the barrier.

After two hundred miles we reach the artificial town of Sharora. It is like an ugly mirage, a pathetic collection of monotonous grey concrete cubes. The only thing growing in this "oasis" is a forest of pylons supporting a tangled canopy of electric cables. Its inhabitants, lost in the dead-end of progress, are like extra-terrestrial creatures roasting alive in an urban hell.

This Bal Harith woman is richly adorned for the sacrificial feast. Western edge of the Rub al Khali.

92

On the northern edge of the Rub al Khali.

It is Ramadan, the month of fasting that marks the end of the Moslem year, and we are heading towards the eastern side of the Rub al Khali, accompanied by our friend Louis le Pivain, a mountain-climber and traveller, who wants to add the desert to his list of accomplishments. Every aspect of this stretch of desert - one of the largest in the world - needs to be examined in order to understand it fully.

Accordingly, we leave Sharora for Harad, passing through the Wadi Dawassir, half-way between Najran and Ryad. This region has undergone a veritable metamorphosis ; the huge green patches surrounded by sand are wheat fields, their round shape determined by a radial irrigation system fed by water pumped up from the water table, one hundred metres below ground. This Brobdingnagian project, which has been a springboard for the fantasies and aspirations of the Saudi people, is producing previously unimaginable harvests from the very sand in which they have always been rooted.

Traces of Bedouin life do persist in this region intent on agricultural development ; patched-up black tents stand next to houses and compounds where dromedaries wander aimlessly. Vessels of the high seas, condemned to coastal navigation. This animal, like the Bedouin, has changed on quitting the desert. The dromedary is losing its intrinsic qualities to become idle and degenerate. Relieved of most of its functions, it moves further and further away from its origins that go back beyond the long migratory treks to the time when it was the mount of warriors.

This transformation taking place under our very eyes is not altogether unconnected to the settling process started up by Abdel Aziz Ibn Saoud before the Kingdom was established. Bedouins alternated their alliances between the future king and rival dynasties, taking the best of both worlds. Ibn Saoud sent Islamic missionaries amongst the nomad tribes to preach the superiority of sedentary life in order to turn the Bedouins away from their "guilty beliefs" and lead them to the "Truth". As soon as he had them under his banner, he set up **hijra** - agricultural colonies situated close to watering places where the settled Bedouins formed a religious brotherhood that also served as a fearsome weapon which Ibn Saoud used to further his conquests and establish the Kingdom of Saudi Arabia.

With water and grass close at hand, it is pointless to seek further.

At Harad, sedentary Bedouins make us welcome under their large black tent, close to a date plantation. They no longer live as nomads but still breed livestock keeping one foot in the desert. These people carry out work that once would have been considered below the dignity of a nomad ; they have a natural disdain for working the land and for the order established by peasants in the oases.

A Bedouin woman has put up a splendid **ruag** in preparation for the feast. Our eyes are immediately drawn to the most decorated section placed on the outside of the tent. With the woman's help we examine the geometric designs on the **ruag**, in black on a white background running along its entire length. The weaver chooses and repeats certain motifs which are occasionally identifiable ; a pair of scissors, an armed man, a dromedary, a perfume-burner, a scorpion, a bird and for the initiated - the **wasm** of the

Dark shadows on the sand. Nafud.

clan. Because their religion forbids representations of living creatures, man and animals are reduced to geometric silhouettes. Generally speaking, all aspects of Bedouin life appear in guised - almost abstract - form. Unfortunately,it was not possible for us to be initiated into Bedouin symbolism. The women are prepared to reveal a few of the terms used for elementary motifs but are reluctant to provide further information on the more subtle aspects. They pretend to have forgotten, preferring to let the beauty of the work speak for itself. Only a few of the elder women appear to understand the significance of the more complex designs.

I try to photograph our hostess in front of her work. She waves at me to stop, afraid that she will be recognized by the **wasm** that appears on several sections of the **ruag**.

This brief exchange is brought to an end by the arrival of her husband. The children kiss their father's nose as a sign of respect. He offers us some coffee. The first stars are making their appearance, glowing with that special radiance peculiar to the desert. They are a reflection of the stylized night sky represented by the black and white checks on the **ruag**.
We decline an offer to sleep under the tent, wanting to make the best of a genuine starry sky.

A family of the Dahm tribe.

Amongst
the Al Murrah people.

We leave Harad on a "corrugated-iron" track marked out by empty barrels. From where the track ends, we can see distant minarets lined up like bayonets ; they seem to be piercing the clouds to bring down the life-saving rain. Yabrin, on the northern tip of the Rub al Khali, is drowsy under the midday sun, like all Arabian towns at this time of the day.

It is open house at the emirate. Anybody can enter, either to make requests and complaints or simply to exchange the latest news.

The Emir receives us courteously. Despite his youth, he accepts the weight of his hereditary title calmly. We are immediately put at ease by his welcome.
The news of our presence must have spread through the town ; the **majlis** is buzzing constantly with inquisitive townsfolk, occasionally joined by the Emir's rebellious-looking young son.
We are delighted to meet a Saudi with a perfect command of English. He works for Aramco in Arabia's largest refinery - Ras Tunura - processing four hundred thousand barrels of crude oil a day. He has come to spend a few days with his parents during Ramadan. We tell him of our wish to explore the eastern side of the Rub al Khali. The idea of going into this desert has never really occurred to him and even though he does not consider this the best time of the year, he would be delighted to accompany us there. He informs the Emir of our conversation who, after learning the reasons for our presence here, invites us to celebrate the end of Ramadan with him and offers to organize an expedition.

We also meet the Regional Administrator whom we convert to our

passion for old objects ; from now on he will frenetically lay his hands on anything old and preserve it, as if out of duty for his tribal heritage. Content to have gained so rapidly the confidence of our hosts, we seek out the Al Murrah Bedouins who have temporarily left this region to escape the summer drought. Where to find them, you may well ask ? The answer is simple - anywhere between Yabrin, north-eastern Saudi Arabia and southern Iraq !

We do our best to avoid civilization but are unable to escape the sight of flares from the refineries. Our dromedaries are forced to straddle or go around an interweaving mesh of pipe-lines. The Saudi's astonishing wealth makes itself felt all around us.
The Arabia I love has got very little in common with what these images evoke - the greed for black gold. Surprisingly, a totally different life can still be found here, a life that was forgotten with the advent of the oil industry.
We have come across an encampment of the Amassir tribe from Abu Dhabi. These nomads, stateless citizens, have been used to cross frontiers in accordance with their needs. Total freedom of travel is one of their most cherished rights.
We examine a collection of curious masks shaped to emphasize the nose. The women of the tribe seem to have forsaken their human nature to become rigid faced birds of prey. Their beauty has been corrupted to escape from men.

Family prosperity was once evaluated from the size of the herd and the dimensions of the tent. Nowadays, an encampment is fitted out with every sort of modern convenience. It is strange to see, in the balmy heat of a

A woman from the Shammar tribe.

Wearing the goatshair head-dress takes a lot of work ! A Yam woman near Najran. (p.100-101)

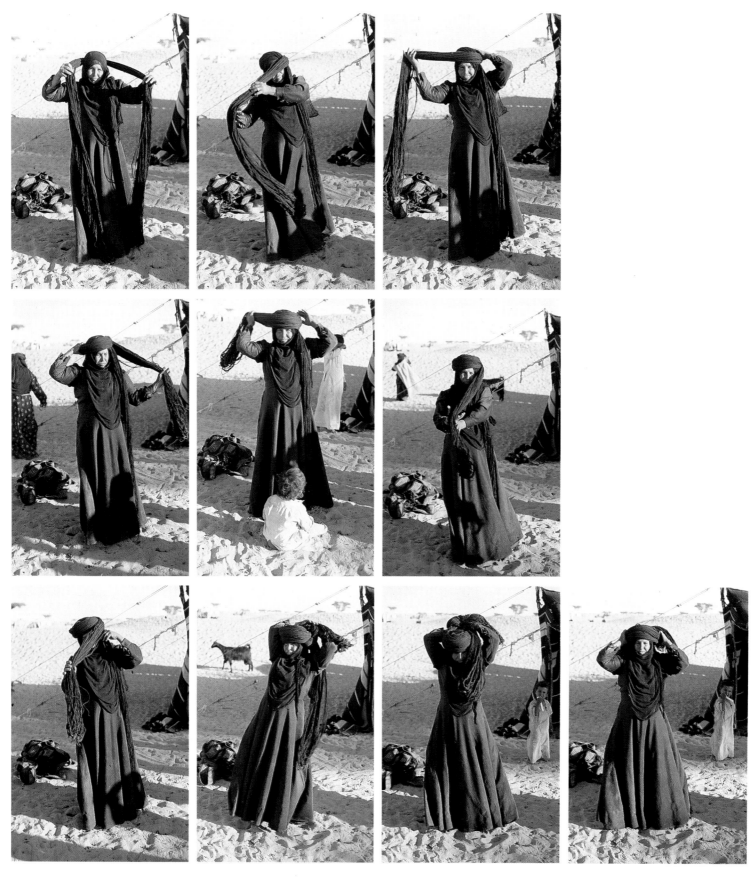

103

tarpaulin tent, a generator, a television set and a refrigerator. A far cry from the time when anything superfluous was discarded. The blessings of civilization are easily loaded onto the truck owned by these wealthy Bedouins, ensuring similar comforts to those found in urban life. In this cultural confusion, goatskin water containers and old brightly coloured bags vaguely recall Bedouin life-style. A water-bag hangs from a tripod ; the water is cooling by evaporation. Our hosts offer us refreshment which, despite their insistence, we are somewhat reticent to accept.

They remind us of the special dispensation for travellers during the month of fasting. Shamelessly we gulp down a can of Pepsi.

Instead of the flames of a welcoming fire, there is only the cold bluish flicker of a television screen. A portable gas cooker stands in for a fireplace. The Bedouin of yesterday watched the immense sea of sand that came to rest at his feet, today he is riveted to the miraculous mirages of the small screen. Can we still speak of the Bedouins or is it a misuse of language ? The Bedouins, as an evolutionary people, adapt to changing circumstance and are thus unavoidably doomed to extinction.

We pass along the Dahna, a strip of dunes stretching over six hundred miles, the junction of the Rub al Khali and the Great Nafud. Eventually, we find the Al Murrah people. Ramadan is not exactly the best time for making contact. The ban on drinking, eating, smoking and enjoying earthly pleasures starts at dawn. To freshen up, the men wrap themselves in wet cloths. At sunset when "it is impossible to tell a black thread from a white one", the fast is broken and everyone makes a dash for the drinks.

The falcon and **saluki** are present at the call, apparently also suffering from the heat. The bird, looking like the god Horus, is perched on a pommel in the sand. Gazelle hunting, with the **saluki** has almost totally disappeared... along with the game. Fauna is becoming increasingly rare with the proliferation of firearms and four-wheel drive vehicles.

One of the old women is running up a dress on an ancient sewing machine. She wears an old-style indigo mask covering her entire face except for her sparkling eyes. This dark blue dye is used to colour clothes and eventually leaves a permanent stain on the skin. Tied to her shawl is a silver triangle - **il-aga** - set off by a turquoise, and an old gazelle horn. This horn was once used for weaving but is now used for untangling hair. The chief proffers his unsteady hand. Since he fell from a camel, his wrist has been giving him trouble. Danielle offers to give him some treatment. She is astonished when her patient ingenuously informs her that this possible fracture is at least five months old ! Danielle does not wish to disappoint him, so she rubs in some ointment and bandages his wrist. The poor man is doubly penalized as it is his socially essential right hand that is injured.

Before leaving, our hosts - thinking it would please us - offer us a bag of **egt**, small hard cheeses with a crumbly texture, not unlike chalk. To their surprise I vigorously decline because, even with the best will in the world, I could not possibly bring myself to eat their little delicacies with a tart milky taste that sets the teeth on edge.

A Shalawah woman prepares butter in a goat-skin churn. (p. 104)

A young Saar is weaned on products of the consumer society... (p. 105).

A palanquin from the Al Murrah of Yabrin.

The feast of Ramadan.

A fine sliver of a crescent moon heralds **Aïd al fitr** - the break of the fast and the beginning of the festivities. It is also our signal to return to Yabrin. The day after our arrival, we are invited under a huge black marquee.

The guests are seated according to rank and status. The Emir sitting in front of a magnificent **ruag**, is wearing a gold-trimmed **abaya*** which emphasizes the elegance of his gestures.

In order to maintain his status a dignitary needs to master the art of handling his **abaya.**

Cars line up in front of the tent. This is the moment when everybody meets up again. Even though they live in town, all the members of the clan come together in these festivities to express their unswerving attachment to the tribe. A young boy respectfully kisses the nose of an elder. Children and adolescents of the elder's line receive a brush of the lips ; meetings with older people or with those of other lineages usually result in a collision of noses. These rituals of welcome are a good illustration of the courteous affection that the Al Murrah of the Al Jaber clan have for each other. As I do not belong to the tribes I am only entitled to a firm handshake.

Next to a huge perfume burner is a coffee scoop, so large that it has been mounted on castors. Everything seems amplified to match the surrounding desert.

Gleaming coffee pots are kept hot on glowing coals in a temporary fireplace made with a few bricks.

Several enthusiastic young boys are granted the honour of attending to and serving the coffee. **Beiz** - coffeepots with leather bound handles and brightly beaded perfume burners are carried around. A sad reminder of the long

---

* **Abaya**, *a coat of black or beige net.*

treks, ceremonial saddles now serve as armrests for the men. They chat together or drink tiny cups of coffee flavoured with cardamon, saffron and cloves.

From a microphone, the **muezzin** calls the faithful to prayer.

The men turn to face Mecca, lying westward beyond the distant dunes. They form a perfect line under the tent and together they offer praise to Allah.

This morning, a number of animals were slaughtered. The early morning calm was shattered by the cries of terrified animals. Their headless carcasses are hung up by their hind-legs and skinned. Their stomachs are slit, spewing out long strings of purple and milky entrails.

Huge plates on legs - **marzuga** - heaped up with rice, mutton, camel meat and huge pieces of steaming fat are placed on the oilcloths that protect the carpets.. Each guest takes some rice, shapes it into a ball and pops it into his mouth, alternating with pieces of meat. The pangs of sympathy that I felt for the animals this morning, are momentarily stifled as I enjoy the succulent dish. Several dignified belches bring the meal to an end.

We return to the Emir's **majlis**. Shoes have accumulated at the entrance. The temperature suddenly changes. As soon as they can afford it, the Bedouins take vengeance on the excessive heat by another excess - the benefits of air-conditioning.

A man plucks a long plaintive cord from his **rebab**. This "desert violin" is made from goatskin sewn onto a wooden framework with a long rough-hewn neck. Following this recital and the inevitable cups of coffee, the guests are permitted to leave their places and retire to the end of the room for a nap.

The oppressive heat outside makes a siesta almost compulsory until late afternoon.

The droning of flies and long periods of idleness start to get us down.

We prefer to take a look around Yabrin. It is more a large village than a town with its houses organized in much the same way as the tents. The layout adheres to the principle of a strict division of space : the space open to men from outside the family and the space reserved for women. To avoid interference, the dwellings have two entrances. We reach the Regional Administrator's house. Three wash-basins stand side by side, outside the door, a sign of notoriety. In the comfortable **majlis**, men are involved in a lively discussion, interrupted while we exchange greetings. Delighted to find somebody he can speak to in English, our host shows off his vocabulary - in much the same way as we do with our arabic ! Bedouins, in general, are not particularly concerned with world problems, as they do not greatly affect their life, but the Administrator makes the best of our presence by bringing us up to date with the little news that has filtered through to Yabrin.

A short distance from Yabrin, the village of Matak is having its own celebrations. Strings of electric lights pierce the night, lighting up an open-roofed **majlis**. The entire male population is gathered around three enormous perfume-burners enjoying the lively festivities.

The once fervent passion for the glory of battle is rekindled in traditional warrior dances. The men have brought out their favourite weapon, the **saif** - a sword decorated with braided knots. The blade is flexible enough to bend both ways. A volley of shots from a Kalachnikov starts up the dance. The men line up in two rows, facing each other. Holding each other by the arm, they sway very slowly from one foot to another. The leader - **rawi** - starts off a short song in honour of the tribe, each group taking up the chorus in turn at the tops of their voices. Eventually, a warrior, brandishing his sword, steps out from each of the groups. The two virtuosi swirl their glinting weapons in a series of figures that suggest the cunning and aggression of battle.

Streaks of summer lightning, the harbinger of rain, put an end to the festival. A short while later, a savage wind blows up, accompanied by a sand storm. Within minutes the entire village is covered in sand. With eyes burning, we leap into our vehicle and head back to Yabrin. We arrive, surrounded by a thick cloud of dust.

Danielle has spent a very different day with the women. There is an atmosphere of elation in their quarters. The women try on new dresses, brought back from the **souk** by their husbands. Wives and young girls are selecting their wardrobes for the festivities from a cascade of multi-coloured silken cloth with floral motifs. A great deal of care is taken with hair. They comb it with a henna and water mix, which strengthens the hair giving it body and sheen. The next day it is rinsed, oiled and then plaited into two or three tresses which are concealed under the mask.

They pay just as much attention to their hands. They are painted with a mixture of henna and rose oil, which eventually turns to brown.

Danielle's white blouse, mauve skirt and her lace underskirt are met by sharp disapproval as Saudis do not like layered clothes which break up the silhouette.

110

Nora takes a huge bunch of keys from her pocket, opens a red wardrobe and presents Danielle with a bundle of cloth - a red dress which she must put on immediately.

Everyone lies down to take a brief siesta. It is only two in the afternoon. A few young children are already sleeping on the huge red carpet.

Danielle is awoken by the commotion of women in the doorway. They stagger under the weight of their adornments, heavy gold breast-plates and innumerable bracelets and rings.

The mistress of the house gives Danielle the place of honour : under the air-conditioner. Each new arrival adds a new touch of colour to the scene, corners of masks are lifted, embraces, greetings. The air is heavy with the sweet smell of amber and incense mixed with that of western perfume.

Two young women wearing masks appear in a flurry of dresses to join this colourful throng of women. They take the veil covering their hair and delicately hold it at arm's length.

They clap their hands to the beat of a whining cassette recorder and start to dance in short steps. One foot follows the other, their hips sway to and fro to the rhythm of the syncopated music, while hands, linked by the veil, accompany the sensually undulating bodies with delicate movements. They turn, eye to eye, cross and turn once more. The music stops. Young children leap in the air, shouting with joy at the opportunity of a break whilst the cassette is rewound.

Preparing to dance, two young girls let out their long tresses and gather up their hair which flows down in a dark cascade with a mahogany glow.

The music starts up again.

With each sway of the head, their slender hands toss their hair back like unfurling veils, covering and uncovering their serious and youthful profiles. This dance of the hair can only be danced by young girls.

Brief power cuts set off a chorus of droning voices from the discreetly impatient women who give a small sigh of relief when the air-conditioner starts up again.

The desert violin.

112

The Rub al Khali expedition.

For some of the elders, our frantic preparations on the morning before our departure stir up wonderful memories of the caravans about to leave. We take special care in checking the jerrycans of water and petrol.

In the old days the traveller's life depended on the watertightness of the **guerba** attached to the animal's sides. Before driving onto the sand, we must reduce tyre pressure. This increases their surface cover and reduces the risks of getting bogged down. It is quite remarkable that a study of the ratio of a camel's weight to the surface area of its feet led to the development of a tyre ideally suited to desert conditions !

The convoy moves off. Since trading our camels for vehicles we have lost the almost intimate contact we had with the dunes and the initiatory nature of desert travel. Our two guides carry all that is required for our survival in their pick-up truck : two hundred litres of water, two hundred litres of petrol, a live sheep and everything needed for cooking. The Emir, the Regional Administrator, a police officer and our friend from Aramco share a second vehicle. We follow as best as we can, the big cloud of dust that blocks our view and invades our nostrils. Our air-conditioner has already given up the ghost, so at least we don't run the risk of catching colds !

We stop for the evening atop a gigantic dune looking out over a gravelly plain. Here, the wind has chosen **sotto voce** for its dialogue with the sand.

We have reached Abu Bahr, the "father of the sea". A Bedouin prepares to slaughter the sheep while we set up camp. With a few heart-rending bleats the poor beast begs our indulgence. In its eyes we can see a desperate "why". By the glow of a lantern, it is dismembered, cut into pieces and tossed into the pot. Within a couple of hours we are dining on the traditional mutton and rice.

One of our guides disappears for a moment and comes back on all fours, his head-cover cleverly arranged to look like two gazelle horns. This comical interlude shows that the initial stage of our journey has already altered our relationship, replacing polite distance with a certain complicity. We soon fall into a deep sleep that nothing could disturb.

We wake up and take a look around. The simplicity of the scenery brings to mind the synthetic images of our computer screens. The remnants of last night's meal are scattered around the bivouac. The Saudis have pointed out that the desert is vast enough not to require rubbish disposal. They do not become attached to the places they pass through. Even though flagrantly indifferent to the environment, they keep their dwelling and their car absolutely spick and span. We leave behind us a mound of sand marked by the stigmata of the consumer society.

For three days we travel four hundred miles exploring the Rub al Khali. The Bedouins and their herds have temporarily deserted these immense arid stretches. With no track in sight we have the feeling of entering into a region where everything remains to be discovered. Space, light, dryness and mineral purity. The same ingredients are endlessly repeated, drawing the traveller into a metaphysical reverie.

Our guides slow down and examine the ground, easily deciphering signs of life that are way beyond our powers of perception. The Bedouins, having learnt the art of survival the hard way,

A woman of the Harb tribe.

114

have a sharp sense of observation and a kind of sixth sense. Reputed for their tracking ability, the Al Murrah can recognize a dromedary and identify its sex from mere tracks in the sand. Without entering into a scatological discourse, the droppings of a dromedary - **damna** - are neither anonymous nor insignificant ; in the hands of these same Bedouins - they turn into identity cards !

Wilfred Thesiger relates the example of a Bedouin who, examining some dromedary tracks, almost obliterated by the wind, picked up a piece of dung, crushed it between his fingers, kneaded it and delivered his verdict : "They were people of the Awamir tribe. There were six of them. They attacked the Junaba on the south coast and took three of their camels. They passed this way about ten days back".

These days, this ability is reaping its rewards ; Al Murrah Bedouins can be found in the Desert Police Force and the National Guard using their talent to full advantage.

In the total emptiness of this flat region, we cannot help but see a solitary tent - a small island of life retaining the charm of a strange lost world.

According to its occupants, we are sixty miles from the nearest encampment. A few sheep, overcome by the heat, are huddled together in the shade of a water bowser, a veritable well on wheels. What necessity has driven a man, a woman and their children to this desolate spot ? They seem to be magicians who have come to give back the desert its life, like astronauts come to colonize a hostile planet.

The sleepy terrain suddenly turns violent : immense gravelly plains - regs, alternate with strips of interm-ingled dunes - ergs, making progress particularly difficult.

Our friends are well aware of what their vehicle can handle and can tell at a glimpse the easiest way through this maze of dunes. They fearlessly attack the first dunes, following their gentle undulations. Like surfers, they appear on the crest of a wave then curving and dipping out of sight come back to shoot another wave that will carry them further.

The treacherous sand quickly brings them to a stop however. The motor growls. We clear huge armfuls of sand from under the wheels. The continuous bogging and the nervous tension from the vertiginous descents leaves us with parched mouths and cracked lips.

Added to the obstinacy of the dunes is the hypothetical presence of water from the life-sustaining wells. They are indicated on the maps by special symbols and their names are clearly marked. They seem impossible to miss. The reality is quite different. Without intimate knowledge of their position, trying to find them in a given area is like attempting to sound infinity. We reach one that has become unusable after being partly filled in by a sliding dune. We have more luck with the Motreba well. 45 metres deep, it has been carefully covered over to keep the sand out. Their masonry coping on which are mounted two diagonal supports and a wooden pulley, the **mahala**, bears the **wasm** of the lineage Kalub. I wind the pulley, it emits a tiny squeak and stops. Leather water skins are scattered around on the ground. Some old saddles, caked by windblown sand are strangely reminiscent of shipwrecks. Enormous amounts of camel dung lie on the sand around the well, a testimony of the life as it once was, of

116

all the herds, of all the men who came here to drink.

In the eyes of a lay observer, the Rub al Khali would appear as a totally desolate region where nothing but a few stunted shrubs grow. We will see that, far from being Proterozoic, the desert is full of surprises !

Although most of its animal inhabitants usually shy away from the sun, the **dhab** seems, on the contrary, to revel under it. He doesn't return to his hole until twilight. The one we surprise takes off abruptly with that great lashing of the tail which has earned it the nickname of whip-tail.

Its salvation lies in retreat. When it gets back to its refuge, the Bedouins smoke out the hole, using twigs, or sometimes a tube leading from a car's exhaust-pipe. The groggy animal is forced to emerge and is easily caught. One of our friends demonstrates a more sporting version. He pulls his **thowb** up to his knees and catches one on the run, grabbing it by the neck. We are able then to examine its strange head, not unlike that of a tortoise.

Suddenly, the car of our two Bedouin guides swerves, zigzags, stops and takes off again like a horse gone berserk. We soon make out the fugitive, a small sand-hare, collapsed from a heart attack after its dreadful ordeal. The hunter, not having had time to sacrifice his victim ritually, will not be including it on the evening's menu and leaves it there.

Further on, a second hare escapes its pursuer. I am secretly pleased. Hunting from cars seems to me far too unjust. I am not the only one to think this way and an argument for and against it ensues. However, group tension becomes almost intolerable under such intensely hot conditions and the dispute is quickly settled.

We see neither gazelle nor antelope as they have been wiped out by hunting safaris. As herdsmen, the Bedouins are radically changing their attitudes towards the fauna. They are different from hunters such as the Eskimo who are very conscious of their dependence on wildlife for their survival and do not kill animals other than out of necessity.

"From dawn to dusk we hunt our prey. And thus its life is filled with terror"

Headlights dance on the horizon, clinging to the increasing number of shrubs and picking out the curved outlines of the gently undulating dunes.

Set up each night, our bivouac provides an almost pastoral charm.

Our guide lights a fire around which social life is always centred. Bedouin life-style is inconceivable, even in the middle of the desert, without the coffee "ceremony". It is one of the few indispensable indulgences in this austere setting. Seated on a carpet of golden dust, the coffee is served with flair, as if in the alluring ambience of a **majlis**. The absence of perfume burners is made up for by placing some incense on glowing charcoal in a sand-filled teacup.

The starry sky has a clarity and magnitude it lacks in the town.

Shooting stars plunge towards the earth presenting a fireworks display well worthy of the location. After being battered all day by the sun, the moonglow is like a soft caress.

With the mind of a polytechnician and the competence of a Tycho Brahe, Louis instructs us in the layout of the heavens.

Heritage of a past civilization : the rocky tombs of Al Ula.

The Return to Yabrin.

After so much time spent in the desert we had almost forgotten the appeal of the oasis. We stop off in the Yabrin palm grove, sunburnt, dirty and worn out. The place has been partially abandoned, leaving pisé houses and palm-leaf huts derelict. At sunset, these sand-choked ruins are a nostalgic sight.

We encounter one old man on his doorstep who was probably around when the palm grove was at the height of its glory. His handsome beard is snow-white and flecked with henna. On his feet he wears the **zarbul** - a type of slipper made from camel hair. Leaning on a saddle, he recounts in vivid detail, Ibn Saoud's visit to Yabrin.
It is well known that the legendary Abdul Azziz came here in 1891 when he was eleven years old, accompanied by his father.
The courage and zeal of this future king of Arabia was strengthened by his tough apprenticeship amongst the Al Murrah people, known as the "nomads of the nomads". The old man's expression shows the pleasure felt by the very old when remembering the part they once had in, what is now, History.
A quick calculation reveals that he was five at the time. He must be a hundred years old now. One more to our credit !
The conversation draws on. The oasis dwellers make the best of our visit to enjoy a few moments of relaxation. One of them cuts an enormous water melon and exposes it briefly to the sun to cool it down by evaporation. Its bright red flesh contrasts sharply with the yellow sand. It is the most delectable refreshment I know.

Leaving our storyteller to his souvenirs of the illustrious visitor, we return to the house of the Emir where he is holding audience. There is a conflict between a Bedouin and a Palestinian, both Yabrin residents. The latter is a local schoolteacher. All community affairs are dealt with publicly in a congenial atmosphere. Anybody can come to make a petition, and offer his opinion on the problem since it is being dealt with communally. Nothing but respect can be felt for this system of justice, carried out in the purest of Bedouin tradition. Each participant galvanizes his own circle into action with an impassioned - and sometimes dramatically inspired - speech.
The Emir's expression alternates between benevolence and severity and then eventually becomes quite serene. After hearing every opinion, he will make a ruling. Although it only involves a run-of-the-mill car accident, it is up to him to afford this affair all the due concern of a traditional institution.

Cave paintings, faithful reminders of old civilizations. Al Ula.

120

About twenty miles from Yabrin, at Al Hafaer, bordering on the dreaded Rub al Khali, my love for old objects has once again been gratified. The invaluable treasures of a past epoch, tents, saddles, packsaddles, water containers, palanquins, are like flotsam in a port at low-tide.

An elderly woman brings one of these relics from her tent for me to peruse at my leisure. The palanquin, **moghbot** is now just a folkloric object, in the hands of a few devotees of the past. Infinitely more elegant than the Yam **tama**, it comprises cradled arches mounted on a saddle which is draped with the luxurious red **shaif**, providing cover from the sun whilst trekking. The tight dimensions of this "gondola" leave us to guess at the size of the women of those bygone days. Once again showing his kindness, the Emir offers to mount the **moghbot** we have purchased on one of his camels. We are to see this antediluvian carcass gradually being adorned with a shimmering skin. Right through the morning the Emir despatches couriers all over town to seek out the missing piece - an authentic **shaif**. But they come back empty-handed.

My palanquin cannot bring back those of the poet :

"On the day of our departure, when our palanquins are strapped tight, they are anemones covered by a misty cloud."

On our way back, we make a stop in the pisé ruins. Several sections of walls emerge from the sand. To convince me that we are standing on an ancient site, our guide invites me to scratch the soil where I soon find some pieces of ancient pottery.

Astonishing sandstone rocks at Medain Saleh.

The feast of the Hadj.

One month later and the time of one of the most significant expressions of Islamic life, the Hadj pilgrimage - the symbol of international Moslem solidarity. At least once in his lifetime every Moslem tries to participate in this pious trek of the ultimate consecration, which confers on him the title of **hadji**. He joins up with the mass of pilgrims that flows into Mecca's immense mosque, dominated by seven giant minarets.
He returns home, touched by divine grace, to receive the esteem of his family, relatives and friends.

We are back in Yabrin, together again for the sacrificial feast which ends the month of fasting. Accompanied by our friend the Emir, we make up a convoy of six four-wheel-drive vehicles and head for Salwah, on the Qatar border, then to Ambak, the fief of the Al Azbah, another clan of the Al Murrah tribe, with whom we are invited to stay.

The usual salaams precede the coffee, tea and incense. We appreciate the performance for the hundredth time - like when watching an old movie which one never tires of, even though every image is predictable. The performance is extended to the cars, decorated with glittering fringes, plastic flowers and tasselled curtains - a symbol of the made-in-Japan modernism that has come to invade Bedouin traditions.
In the shade of the tent, I try my hand at **andara** - a simplified version of draughts played on a twenty four square checker-board provided by holes in the sand. Each player alternately moves one of his six pieces - either pieces of camel-dung or short sticks-without crowning. A pastime well adapted to the debilitating heat.

After this relaxing interlude, we take a look around the area. Our hosts enthusiastically approve of the sentiment we nurture for Bedouin traditions. I am only allowed to spend some time with the women after firmly promising not to photograph them...

An old weather-beaten Bedouin squatting by his vehicle is scanning the tree-tops with his powerful binoculars. His falcon has got away and is perched on a branch scoffing at his master. Frustrated, the man tries to coax him with a bait of sheep entrails, but the falcon refuses to return to his master's wrist. He is thoroughly enjoying his newly-found freedom.

Sunset and time for prayer.
Under the tent, a superb banquet brings us all together. Our hosts, showing that they are familiar with European customs, offer us cutlery. We refuse and, to show that we are trying to adapt to their customs, we awkwardly attempt to knead a ball of rice in our palms.
Our sleeves rolled up to the elbows, we wash the rice from our right hands under a trickle of water.

The meal is followed by a salvo of automatic rifles and warrior dances. The men take up aggressive postures to fire their guns at full blast. Children pick up the still warm spent shells. The Emir joins the dance, sword on the back of his neck, in a similar manner to shepherds who carry their stick across their shoulders to ease the back while walking long distances. Other men join him, their swords drawn. And the verbal sparring begins...

When the festivities are ended, we go back to our overnight quarters among the dunes, overlooking the town.

The entrance of the Medain Saleh sanctuary.

124

Dawn is just breaking and the camp is already being dismantled. The cars leave, bumper to bumper, for the race course. The top cameleers of the region are to be put to the test over a 15 kilometre track. Ten splendid racing camels await the starter's signal. A confused medley of cars follows the camels, making it look more like a stock car race. Their necks stretched out in front of their bodies, side legs moving in unison, they seem to be defying the laws of gravity.

Proudly seated in his ultra-light racing saddle, the jubilant winner poses for photographs then jumps down from his frothy-mouthed mount to join the Emir who presents him with a dagger and a substantial cheque.

The fiery-spirited racing camel is difficult to handle. A Bedouin narrowly escapes being bitten by a camel while dragging him to the top of a dune. A pick-up truck is driven up to the slope to load on the camel. It takes the strength of several men to bring the champion to task. After the glory of the race, he is not too happy to find himself on the back of a truck !

Rock tomb on a pre-Islamic Nabatean site at Medain Saleh.

A Harb elder beneath her tent. (p.128-129)

Journey's end.

Having taken leave of our friends, we make a short stop at Hofuf. This ancient town was once the Eastern capital - now replaced by the oil capital of Dammam. We follow the Dahna in the north of Juda where we are surprised to come across several Iraqi encampments. Apparently it is not unusual to meet Iraqi Bedouins who have come here to find better pastures. The use of truck transport has made their movements a lot easier.

Night has already fallen as we approach Riyad. The sudden confrontation with this megalopolis of the future after being immersed in the sources of desert civilization makes us feel quite dizzy ! What to make of this sprawling city ? For how long can it be drip-fed on black gold...

At the end of a six hundred mile road stretching across the Najd - a pastoral steppe region with the occasional oasis - we arrive back in Taif. On the road we passed long strings of trucks decorated like Christmas trees.
They pass through the desert, transporting the germs of acculturation...

A "Shisha" Bedouin smokes his pipe (p. 130)

The long lineage... from the dromedary to the four-wheel drive (p.130)

The best of both worlds : modern acquisitions and life under the tent (p.131)

Journey's end with the Atawi.

The end of a long trek ?

In the meeting between two societies, it is the weakest that is usually destroyed. Western influences worm their way into Bedouin life and erode its traditional values.
Out of place in the midst of a new technological environment, everything is working against them.

These last images illustrate the constant fusion of two separate entities and confirm the feelings I have had all along this journey.

Although pastoral nomadism in its secular form is irrevocably condemned, other types of nomadic life, more adapted to our society, could very well emerge.
Unstable employment, short-term contracts, expatriation, mobile homes are becoming widespread out of sheer economic necessity. If this trend continues, the resulting migratory movements could lead to Bedouin-like behaviour, its rituals and its ethics.

Will this trend be a forerunner of the long-lost freedom for which each man secretly craves ? Some have already begun the search.
As nomads among the Bedouins we bear the seeds of this new nomadism.

To all Bedouins I asked this fundamental question :
"Do you want to pursue your nomadic life or do you want to settle for good ?"

The answer came as a heartfelt cry :
"We want to LIVE !"

Twilight of the Bedouins in the Rub al Khali.

134

Bibliography.

The following bibliography is relatively short since I have tried to place emphasis on our personal experiences and impressions, in preference to working from a large number of, often outdated, reference books on the Bedouins of Arabia.

- BONNENFANT Paul, "L'évolution de la vie bédouine en Arabie centrale". Sociological notes. Extract from the Revue de l'Occident Musulman et de la Méditerranée. N23, 1977.
- OUCHEMAN Albert de, "Matériel de la vie bédouine". Ethnographic Museum, 1934.
- CHELHOD Joseph, "Le droit dans la société bédouine". Marcel Rivière. Paris, 1971.
- COLE Donald Powell, "Nomads of the nomads. The Al Murrah bedouin of the Empty Quarter". Aldine Publishing Co. Chicago, 1975.
- DICKSON H.R.P., "The Arabs of the Desert". Allen and Unwin. London, 1949.
- DOUGHTY Charles, "Arabia deserta". Extracts translated by Garnett and Marty, Payot. Paris, 1949.
- JAUSSEN Antonin, "Coutumes des Arabes au pays de Moab". Adrien Maisonneuve. Paris, 1948.
- MAUGER Danielle et Thierry, "A l'ombre des tentes noires". Tihama. Ryad, 1986.
- THESIGER Wilfred, "Le désert des déserts". Terre Humaine. Plon. Paris, 1978.